HEAVEN AWAITS

YOUR *EXPRESSION*

*One Man's Breathtaking Experience with
Jesus in Heaven*

BROCK E. KNIGHT

Heaven Awaits Your Expression

Copyright © 2020 Brock E. Knight All rights reserved

The characters and events portrayed in this book are described to the best of the author's ability. Any similarity to real persons, living or dead, is coincidental and not intended by the author.

No part of this book may be reproduced, or stored in a retrieval system, or transmitted in any form or by any means, electronic, mechanical, photocopying, recording, or otherwise, without express written permission of the publisher.

ISBN-13: 9798583701810

Cover design by: Brock Knight
Printed in the United States of America

TreeHouse Publishers
www.treehousepublishers.com
www.gotreehouse.org

Contact Author:
Brock E. Knight
134 1st Ave NW
Winchester, TN
www.BiblicallyWhole.com
www.watb.tv
brock@watb.tv

Heaven Awaits Your Expression

TABLE OF CONTENTS

INTRODUCTION: PG V

CHAPTER 1: HEAVEN'S COLORS   PG. 1

CHAPTER 2: EYES LIKE STARS   PG. 23

CHAPTER 3: MY GUARDIAN ANGEL   PG. 41

CHAPTER 4: THE FATHER'S GLORY   PG. 55

CHAPTER 5: THE TREES, FLOWERS, & WATER   PG. 61

CHAPTER 6: THE HEAVENLY JERUSALEM   PG. 77

CHAPTER 7: THE TREES IN EDEN   PG. 95

CHAPTER 8: THE ANIMALS IN HEAVEN   PG. 105

CHAPTER 9: BRICKS OF GOLD   PG. 113

CHAPTER 10: JAMI'S MANSION   PG. 129

CHAPTER 11: JESUS GLORIFIED   PG. 145

CHAPTER 12: THE LIBRARY OF WISDOM   PG. 161

DEDICATION

To the Lord Jesus, who has saved me and still abides with me despite all of my weakness. You have truly shown me that YOU are in me and you are my prize and highest calling! It is no longer I who lives, but Christ in me!

To my loving, beautiful, and supportive wife Laura: You have been with me from the beginning. Thank you for bearing His cross with me and charging ahead into new territory! You are the closest example of God's love, purity, & grace in our family's life every single day. Thank you and I love you! Te Amo!

To all my children: Daniel, Catalina, Samuel (in the womb now), Joseph (next one in the womb), & all the others we pray we can adopt in the future! We are amazed at the expression of God we see in you every day!

To my son Daniel: You make me extremely proud to be called a father. You are the example to all other young men of what it means to fear God in your youth. You are a leader like Daniel in Babylon! May young men around the world follow your example of kindness, respect, & wisdom. I will always be there for you! Love you!

To my mother Dr. June Knight: You have been there as long as my guardian angel has. You've watched, guarded, and stood at the gates all of my life to ensure that this message would one day get out to the whole world. You deserve honor, and my gratitude, all the days of my life. May my family and all the families of your children always rise and call you blessed! Love you!

Heaven Awaits Your Expression

REVIEW

Bride,
    Thank you so much for reading Brock's book. As I read it I cry remembering when he was born. I remember when he was filled with the Holy Ghost speaking in tongues for two days at five (5) years old. I remember Jesus coming to see him every five (5) years of his life. I saw him at ten years old on the floor wailing and crying before the Lord speaking in tongues. I remember the persecution he's been through in his life. I know who Brock E. Knight really is. I am a testimony to his life that this experience you're about to read is a real legit story. I can bear witness that when he was growing up he saw many miracles with God. He has been through a lot and now that the Lord took him to Heaven this year (2020), I believe it is to ensure us on what is about to happen in our world. I believe he is assuring us that all of this is temporary and what we have to live for is eternal.
    I also believe that God is wanting us to live out our full expressions of who He is. Not the expression the world has defined and come up with…but one that requires full obedience.
    I pray this book changes your life. It sure did mine.

Dr. June Knight
White House Correspondent
Mother to Brock & Mother to Many in the Body of Christ
We are the Bride Ministries
134 1ˢᵗ Ave NW
Winchester, TN 37398

Heaven Awaits Your Expression

INTRODUCTION

It all started on a Sunday afternoon. It was January 12th, 2020 at our small farm in Grayson, Georgia; just east of the largest city in the Southeast United States - Atlanta. My wife Laura and I found ourselves cozied up on our couch on a cold winter day. I can still remember the scene clearly. The room was beautiful. The atmosphere was just how we like it. Peace reigned in the air. It was glowing, light was reflecting throughout the room, and the stone wall around the fireplace was facing back at me. We were smiling, feeling grateful, and discussing the finer points of why we believe the Christmas tree should stay up all year long! Yes, it was still standing bright, in the corner across the way. We just took it in. It was nothing but the sounds of quietness in our ears.

We enjoyed the stillness, calm, and respite of the moment. We pulled the blanket over our cold toes and began to thank the Lord for the time. We had just successfully laid our three-month-old baby girl to sleep. We knew the nap would only last for 30-45 mins and it was everything Laura could do to enjoy the moment before she too would drift off into her pregnant comatose. It was all too familiar of a routine…it was the calm, the moment to reflect, talk, and drift away before it was go-time all over again. This day, however, was going to end differently than we expected.

There was something bubbling up within me. We were overflowing with the life of God after worshipping that morning at church. We had one of those mornings where we just wept before God. It was a full spirit, soul, mind, & body exertion of energy wholly toward our Heavenly Father that morning. It was an amazing time in worship with fellow believers. We just flowed with the Lord. It was no longer songs being sang by a worship leader. It was the Spirit of God gushing out of everyone, the spontaneous worship from each individual, flowing upwards, and out of their bellies towards our Christ!

Heaven Awaits Your Expression

Once we got back to the house after church, we were going through the plans as Laura had to go see her family. First, we had to take care of the girl, eat, chores on the farm, and Catalina needed a nap. It was a normal Sunday afternoon.

Inside of me though, there was a deep stirring. I knew I was going to get the house to myself later. I could sense the Spirit was wanting that time for Him...and Him alone.

As I sat there on the couch with Laura, that same gushing desire was still bubbling up within my soul. I felt like I could just cry at any moment. I just knew the Spirit wanted me to get alone with Him.

I told Laura, "Babe, I feel like the Lord wants me to just worship Him. I feel like He's wanting to say something to us."

Laura responded, "Yeah, I feel that too...but I think I'm going to fall asleep...ahhh, you just pray, and I'll agree. You lead."

I just held her in and smiled. This was expected. She was totally going to be out in 3...2...and there she goes! She was out. The kind of cold turkey fall asleep as you talk, sort of drifting away, that mothers alone can understand.

Limited with my ability to do much with Laura leaning on me, I grabbed the tv remote with my free hand. I navigated through and started some beautiful instrumental worship on the Roku tv. I turned the volume up a little more, put the remote down, and breathed in. I breathed out.

"Father, here I am."

"Jesus, You are worthy. Thank you for this day. Thank you for my family Lord. I bless your name. I magnify your name. Jesus, you are HOLY. HOLY. HOLY..."

Just as I normally would begin my typical time alone with the Lord, it began. I routinely honed in my senses to become aware of the Holy Spirit. I felt the urge inside.

I focused and took my mind off myself, my day, my worries, and the list of things to do. I simply blessed His name, gave Him praise, thanked Him, and I yielded.

I was feeling the well of living water starting up. I found myself singing louder. It was in English. Then in tongues.

Heaven Awaits Your Expression

I was flowing from singing, "Holy, Holy, Holy, is your Name," and then back to my prayer language. This was going somewhere. This was when I realized the Lord had an agenda. I had better get in line. It was happening.

I just kept flowing with the Lord. I was singing, then crying, then my hands were raised, my volume was up, energy was up, and before you know it- I was standing. Laura was out on the couch and I was just feet away experiencing His joy, His sweet peace, that warm powerful Love flowing in and out of me. I was in the Spirit. I was in the zone (some would say). I was in the moment and my heart was pounding with excitement and expectancy of what the Lord would do or say. I continued on…

Then, the voice of the Lord, speaking from within my spirit loud & clear, whispered inside, "Brock, listen. Listen."

I quieted myself, sniffled the snot, and stood still in my living room. The music playing was a piano version of the song, *"Let it Rain"* and I distinctly remember it keying the part of the song where it sings, "Open the floodgates of Heaven…. Let it Rain!"

The piano played some more. It was the sweetest of moments. It's when you feel that personal intimacy with your King. It's a personal culmination of years of experience worshipping the Lord, knowing when He is near, and submitting your mind & soul to Him in that moment.

I stayed silent. Still. I could hear and feel only my heartbeat.
I heard the Lord.
"Brock"
I heard Him continue, "Brock, get your laptop. Sit down. I want you to write down everything you see."

Then I was pulled out of the moment.

That's right, I heard the baby crying! Laura woke up. It was time to get them ready to head out to the family get together at the in-laws. I lovingly helped them get packed up, loaded into the car, and kissed them goodbye for the afternoon.

Heaven Awaits Your Expression

I could not wait to get back into the room with the Lord and continue, so I did all my chores on the farm as fast as I could. I fed the chickens, watered the cows, and played with Rocky. I worshiped the Lord and thanked Him every single bit of time out there!

—An hour later—

It was not long after, and I was sitting on the couch worshiping the Lord with my laptop in my lap and ready to type. That's when it began to flow out of me. I was seeing the start of a vision in my imagination. I felt the Spirit highlight the phrase, where it says to have the "eyes of your understanding being enlightened" as the Apostle Paul spoke of in Ephesians 1.

I could see the Christmas tree still, the stone wall around the fireplace too. Across the open room was the distant wall of windows with the setting sunlight and the fog of winter being apparent. The light of the Christmas lights glowed still. The music still played. I was still seeing everything in the natural. I was aware.

So there I was, sitting there, staring at the Christmas tree. Looking at the dazzling lights wrapping the tree, the reflecting ornaments, and the stillness it had.

I began to center in on the light flooding into my imagination. I heard a repeat of what the Lord had spoken to me about five minutes ago. He had said to me, "Brock, I'm flooding the eyes of your imagination with light" referring to Ephesians 1:17-18.

Five minutes of being lost in imagination, I stared at the tree, until the light was subtly bringing my attention to the start of a LIVE daydream/vision forming in my spirit. I began to yield to the thought, the imagination, the movie playing. The same faculty of my mind used to play vivid movie like dreams when I'm asleep was now functioning as I sat there.

Heaven Awaits Your Expression

It was as if I had an inner remote to play, pause, and slow it down if need be. I sensed it coming. I was getting used to this inward media player. I let the video start. I knew a vision was before my mind's eyes.

It is a bit like the days when you were in school and the teacher was talking on and on, but you were in a distant la-la land inside your mind's imagination. You were playing this drama out in your mind so much so that your heart rate went up, you jumped when the bad guy came at you, and you reflexively moved your arms. Then you realized the teacher was calling your name! You snap out of it and try to come back to Earth and reality!

We have all experienced daydreaming. That's basically the simplest way to describe a vision.

You can have a vision of the night when you sleep (also called a dream) or you can have a vision in the day (some call it day dreaming). I was having a Spirit inspired day vision. If you've ever operated in the prophetic and allowed the Lord to use you to speak an inspired word to another person, then you may have experienced seeing a picture, idea, or having a "knowing" about something you are to tell the receiving person. This is the same operation by the Spirit. He speaks to you in the "spirit of your mind" (Eph. 4:24) and uses your imagination as the movie screen to show you something He is saying.

~

Jesus was there. I could hear Him saying, "Brock, come here. Let me show you Heaven."

I could sense Him standing there to my front right, I could sense His hand waving before Him. I had a dim view of something before me. It was land and sky.

That was not capturing all of my attention, but oddly enough, the darkness behind me was. I didn't think to look back and study the darkness, because all of this was all rapidly forming into thoughts within my mind. But I sensed darkness behind me and light before me. Was I at the outskirts of Heaven?

Heaven Awaits Your Expression

Jesus said, "Would you like me to show you Heaven? I'd like you to come with me. Are you ready?

I was hearing Him saying this, and yet I was still thinking in my head, "Is this me imagining this? Is this truly You speaking to me Lord?" I was just starting to enter in, and it was as if the more I tried to focus in, it was clearer. If I decided to take my mind away from this, details would dim away.

I could sense Jesus smiling in an understanding way. His thoughts were in me. He knew I couldn't see anything. I just heard him whisper, "Come with me, and I'll show you Heaven. I've got much to show you.

~

Get ready. This book should cause you to have frequent moments of discovery about your Heavenly Father, Jesus, the Holy Spirit, and all of the hosts of His Creation.

My advice to you. Take this moment to eliminate all the distractions. Give yourself enough quiet time to hear the Lord talk to you throughout these pages. Don't treat this as a typical novel, DIY, or self-help book. Ask the Lord to speak to you and renew your mind. Ask Him to conform you into His image.

The days are short. The time is at hand. The end is here. We are living in the final days. Judgment is upon the world.

We are seeing prophecies fulfilled every day. It is coming...the day you will have to choose martyrdom or compromise. You will either join the ranks of the comfortable and cowardly or stand on streets of gold and walk by Jesus in Glory. Please, I am asking you as a friend and a brother, allow me to walk you through my experience with Jesus in Heaven.

All I ask is that you keep a few thoughts within the forefront of your mind. I am just a brother and anything I can do; you can do as well. Any experience I have had, you can as well. Don't think more highly of me than you ought to think.

Heaven Awaits Your Expression

The mind-blowing displays of God's Glory is not just for my eyes only. You too will see all that I have seen.

I'm not special and the only one privileged to see these things. Your day is coming soon. You too will stand with Jesus. You will see His eyes. You too will experience the awe and dread of falling down before God Almighty. There is no respecter of persons with Him. If He will do this with me, then He can do this with any believer who desires the same. I pray that you will open your eyes and your heart to experience the colors of Heaven with me. Let's begin.

Fitting for this moment, is the song my mom Dr. June Knight always sings:

"What a day,
that will be,
when my Jesus
I will see"

CHAPTER 1

HEAVEN'S COLORS

"It was colors... colors.... clouds of glory all in a white blaze from the center and pulsating outward!"

"Brock, Take My hand, let Me take you into that water."

At this point, I was seemingly distracted with the realities of Jesus speaking to me. He described what was in front of me as water. I wasn't sure if it was a veil...an entrance...I'm not sure. I was only seeing dimly. All I could process mentally about my environment was coming in slowly. I could make out vaguely the light, a sky, something like water, and what seemed to be people before me. Behind me was nothing but pure darkness. I felt like I was at the very edge of Heaven. Or was I?

I did what was told of me. I reached out. I felt His hand. Wow! I could feel! I could sense emotion inside me slightly. Ok, this is getting clearer.

I followed silently forward at the hand of Jesus. I started to see some appearance of light ahead and what looked like a pool of sparkling energized fizzing water. I just tried to will my eyes to see more.

I was thinking, "ugh, come on eyes...see! Look further. I wanted to see the clouds of Heaven! What was the Throne like?

Heaven Awaits Your Expression

What would the colors around His throne look like? Is this happening? Oh please, let me see Heaven!" All of these thoughts were instantly simultaneously coming through my mind.

Within the same second of thought, I began to remember, that I was with Jesus! I started to turn to look at Him!

Oh, I get to see Jesus? What! Oh, is this only my mind? Is this my imagination?

I was turning my eyes to Jesus, and He was there! He was hard to make out! Now I'm really thinking that my eyes need to see. I need to focus my eyes on His face! I want to see…but my eyes were only seeing His hand and arm. I knew His person was there, but all else was dimmed but the arm of Jesus!

At this time, we made it to the edge of this water. It was the slowing and peaceful swirl of a stream that somehow pooled up into a perfect active belly deep swimming area. It reminded me of a swimming hole from the creeks I swam in as a child growing up in the country hills of Tennessee.

I was on a walkway. This walkway was leading right into the pool of water created by the sparkling stream. I couldn't make out the stream's details because of the dimming of my eyes. But I could see a measure of pretty light coming through.

I could not see details well past the water either. I could make out within the light I was seeing that the pathway we were walking on was continuing forward into the water. A detail not noticed earlier…the path wasn't grass anymore. It was an orange-ish color. Hold up. Gold! Straight out of the water pooling peacefully in a gentle swirl, was a pure smooth polished golden pathway. Not bricks. Not slabs. One solid paved gold sheet. It was like a solid roll of gold rolled out as a pathway. It began to register. I truly was with Jesus.

Now, even though the gold was beautiful…I was brought back to the moment. Jesus was stepping into the water.

I noticed part of his robe was coming into my vision. IT WAS PURE WHITE. I saw a glimpse of gold clothing. Clothing made of gold! I have never seen that on Earth!

Heaven Awaits Your Expression

~

Ok, maybe I am in Heaven. I'm becoming convinced now. I decided to continue on with this. It seemed as though I was imagining this myself at first. Quickly, I realized that He was bringing me into "seeing Heaven" and I committed to following Him. I decided inwardly I was not letting go of this! I was going to sit right here and stare continually at the same spot…at the Christmas tree…and follow every single bit of this!

~

Jesus stepped in, and stepped again, His robe was fascinating me now. Is it getting wet? It wasn't exactly moving to my expectations. It reacted differently to the water. The water was completely energized.

As I was watching and noticing details, I tried to look down to watch where I was stepping. With all my experience of walking in creeks, I've been so aware of rocks jarring my feet and sharp pains, cuts, and scrapes. I wasn't allowed to see. I just saw my foot in the water.

My next thought was, "Oh this water is fizzing all over my foot and leg. It's massaging me. Oh, this feels wonderful!

The water wasn't clouding up with algae, dirt, or any disturbance at all. Cool! I could see the water dancing, swirling, and rippling outward like I expected it to…just differently. The ripples were dancing outwardly. The water was beautiful. It was so clear. It was clearer than glass. It was way more than "crystal clear" and beyond my experience on Earth. It seemed as though it was not capable of being dirty at all. Wow. This was different than Earth! I've never seen such beautiful water!

There seemed to be gold underneath. Ok, that made sense. The gold from the path is continuing through the water.

I cannot believe how much I could think in such a split second of time!

Jesus and I peacefully walked out into the center of the pool. I was noticing more details.

Heaven Awaits Your Expression

We were heading in the direction toward what seemed to be Heaven…which is the most obvious conclusion I could come up with. Brilliant. I laughed to myself.

I willed my eyes to see across the water again. What was over there? Nothing was clear to my eyes, but an inward knowledge of what was behind. I knew there was a city beyond what I could see currently. Mountains behind. Trees. Light. Clouds. Oh, I wanted to see!

Something else dawned upon me…actually, someone! Standing on the other side of the stream, on the pathway, were two figures. I could see them standing dimly, at attention, with their arms folded across their chests. They waited for me? Were they someone I knew?

All of those thoughts stopped. I was in the moment with Jesus. He said, "Brock, this is the water that allows you to see what you want to see. This is what I must do. You cannot go forward until you are brought through this water."

He took me, as if baptizing me. I was facing the two beings in front of me, the city of God before me, and Jesus to my right. He placed one hand on my chest and one on top of my head. He took me under, going forward.

I was in the water.

The energy of the water woke me up! Not a cold chilled affect like I am used to on Earth. It was a human warmth. The water felt like an embrace. It felt like a hug of energized refreshment to my spirit, soul, & body. So fresh! "FRESH" was the thought coming to me. It instantly felt like mountain air. Mountain fresh air right there under the water! Perhaps it breathes and is full of oxygen? I don't know. I just know that I feel like I'm deep in the depth of untouched wilderness! I'm feeling the most refreshing, soul awakening, mountain crisp air within this water!

Jesus held me there a few moments. Oh, I didn't want to leave the water! I instantly thought of what it will be like when I come out of the water. "I need to wipe my eyes" is my thought now. I have contacts. My contacts will come loose and come out in water.

Heaven Awaits Your Expression

I said to myself, "Wait, my eyes are open. Open underwater!" I knew that opening my eyes under water with my contacts in is bad.

My contacts are done! Gone! But that wasn't the case at all. How silly of me. I had no need of contacts here!

I came up from the water next. I was instantly out of the water and standing up on the golden walkway. I looked over to my right, and I saw grass! Unimaginably GREEN grass! Green green. Like green with LED lights imbedded within the grass…it was registering. It was as if the landscaping had lights imbedded into each plant.

I looked then to the right and behind me. There was the water. It was like the sun was shining at a perfect angle and the light was reflecting off of the sparkling water surface right into my eyes. My head reacted and my eyes widened. It was as if my eyes were taking in more light than ever! My eyes!

I was startled! I turned quickly to see if my eyes were working! I was oblivious to all standing around me. I opened my eyes and looked all around me. I looked back toward the brightest of all the light.

Before me, as if I was perhaps hundreds of miles away, and yet close, was what I was desiring to see all my life! I would spend hours reading Isaiah's vision of the Throne, Ezekiel, Jesus's Transfiguration, John's descriptions in the Book of Revelation, the Gospels, Moses's experiences in the Torah, etc. I have always wanted to see this! Oh, the emotion welling up inside of me. I was in shock and just giddy with an un-matched feeling of privilege that I've never experienced!

I looked up! I saw glimmering clouds. I think they were clouds. I could make out the movement of the clouds. It looked like clouds.

I started to roll through the catalog of descriptive pictures…all of my Earthly words and knowledge- what could describe the clouds?

How do I describe what I was seeing? I was stopped. Everything seemed to stop. I was not able to think. I just had one thought at a time. I was zapped of all other life or activity around me. All I could hear was the word "color" in my mind. I was star struck.

Heaven Awaits Your Expression

Yeah, that's the best word I can say at this very moment. Oh, the color! It was colors...colors.... clouds of glory, all in a white blaze from the center and pulsating outward!

It was almost what looked like bursts and streams and waves and rings and clouds and what looked like the most beautiful star I've ever seen!

I can only explain it like looking at a Nebula Star or a Supernova image you can find from NASA. The Hubble Telescope type of images! Google it! Look up nebula, supernova, or the birthing/dying of a star. The explosion of a star. That's close to what I was seeing. It was some radiant bursting brightness. It seemed to have the effect of imploding energy.... explosive, consuming, ferocious energy.

I just let my eyes rest on the Brightest of Lights I've ever seen. Oh, it was like lightning white. It was only bearable to look at because of the dust of color around Him. It was certainly the Throne of God. Wait, that wasn't the Throne- that was HIM! I couldn't see the Throne at all. All I could see was the Brightness in the center, and rings of colorful glory waves flowing outward. He was the greatest sight I've ever beheld. I could discern similarities to that of a colorful galaxy. It reminded me of how some galaxies swirl. Like that of a hurricane, or the top clouds of a tornado.

My brain was firing on so many levels. Everything I beheld was being processed with information I've acquired throughout my whole life. I was seeing nanosecond videos, pics, thoughts, explanations, and scripture to fully understand everything I looked at. I was thinking rapidly and sharply- in the most impressive quickness! Perhaps this is how our minds work in Heaven?

I had the **Ezekiel 1:4 (KJV)** scripture flowing through my understanding:

⁴ And I looked, and, behold, a whirlwind came out of the north, a great cloud, and a fire infolding itself, and a brightness was about it, and out of the midst thereof as the color of amber, out of the midst of the fire.

I was looking at the Glory of Almighty God and the revelation blowing up in my new heavenly mind was overwhelming me.

Heaven Awaits Your Expression

How can I put Him into words? Lord help me! His person wasn't completely in form where I was looking from. I could just tell from some internal knowing, that there was a mountain of sorts. Was God the mountain?

Oh, I couldn't tell! He was as I would imagine the largest sun in any galaxy or universe out there in the cosmos! I'm talking about a Sun! He had to be the largest of suns. Perhaps I was more than hundreds of thousands of miles away! First of all, how could I determine distance like that? Wow…this is beyond me!

He was what I would imagine it would look like to be beholding the birthing of a sun star. The energy pulsating from all the fusion of many, many, many stars, light, and whatever gases are mixing to make stars! The clouds of dust, or glory, that radiated so much color was no doubt the effects of His radiant energy!

Scientifically, I think He must have some kind of dynamic fusion going on! Oh, I can't describe it with the right quantum terminology! I'm not a scientist at all. But in that split second, the miracle of being able to use my whole mind's processing abilities was just unbelievable!

But the Star of all stars…the Sun in brightness that has birthed all existing stars! He Himself was a galaxy before my eyes! He was His own nebula of light radiating colors beyond my description! The colors were so beyond our world that I gawked and gazed at the clouds and particles of what looked like a brilliant display of many stars scattered throughout the sky!

The sky was so brilliant! There was no nighttime star filled skies on planet Earth quite like these! But yet, it was close to the same thing. This was so magnificent! The wonder it all had me in. I was captured by the endless amount of detail to take in!

Then it hit me! "My eyes! My eyes! The light! I can see all these colors! Lord, I can see the light! This is Heaven! That's the Throne of God…or I'm seeing God the Father from here! I can see Him! The water, it changed my eyes! I can see the sky!

I can see the sun setting…wait. Hmmm…" I stopped to reconsider what this would be called in Heaven. I tried to be more accurate, and tried again saying, "I can see His light reflecting on everything!"

There were no sun sets in Heaven. There was just a constant eternal colorful sunset effect on the sky.

Imagine the most beautiful sunset you've ever seen. Now, remember all the hues of colors? The orange, the purple, blues, reds, the pinks, etc. all mixed into one beautiful painting in the sky. That's close to what it's like in the skies of Heaven!

It must've been the Spirit of God inside of me bearing witness to everything I was seeing. I was having scriptures flowing into my mind. A few remained strong throughout my whole time there:

Psalm 97:6 (KJV)
> **⁶ The heavens declare his righteousness, and all the people see his glory.**

Psalm 8:1 & 3-4 (KJV)
> **¹ …who hast set thy glory above the heavens.**
>
> **³ When I consider thy heavens, the work of thy fingers, the moon and the stars, which thou hast ordained;**
>
> **⁴ What is man, that thou art mindful of him? and the son of man, that thou visitest him?**

Hebrews 12:29 (KJV)
> **²⁹ For our God is a consuming fire**

1 Tim 6:16 (KJV)
> **¹⁶ Who only hath immortality, dwelling in the light which no man can approach unto; whom no man hath seen, nor can see: to whom be honour and power everlasting. Amen.**

I continued to process what I was seeing. There was what looked like a mountain where the Father was radiating. It was a seemingly small slope upward towards the center. I don't know how I knew

Heaven Awaits Your Expression

He was at the center...I just did. It was only a gentle slope that went up from where
I was all the way to the thundering area in the center. It seemed like the golden path I was on led straight to the Throne of God!

My eyes were amazing! I could see all of this! I didn't need glasses or contacts like on Earth.

My eyes seem to gauge distance, zoom in, and basically see what I wanted to see and see how close I wanted to as well. I was able to see up close near the Father's light.

I could make out some walls that seemed many miles high! I perceived what seemed to be what could only be the temple before the Father's and Jesus's Thrones. I saw the most magnificent walls. These walls looked like no other on Earth. These walls were what could only be processed by my mind as many miles high, possibly one solid stone, and made of the rarest gems, gold, granite/marble looking stone, etc.

I'm telling you this, I'm not an expert on stones, gems, and precious metals. But with my eyes, I could see that it was all that we had on Earth and more mixed together to make what seemed to be one solid slab for many miles high and an untold number of miles long. I can't explain that at all. But what I can tell you is this. That wall screamed loud in my knowing as SECURITY. It was clear that you cannot go past that wall without permission.

What caught my eye as well were the trees surrounding that particular wall. Trees that were thousands of feet tall! Trees and vines that seemed to grow with the wall. It looked so ancient and created to be the landscape around the wall!

The wall had these huge sections where water was flowing through it and around it. Oh, I willed my eyes to see the details (all of this happening in the shortest of time) and I couldn't take in the details.

I wanted to follow the water though! I looked up and I followed the most beautiful of rivers, waterfalls, and perfectly landscaped water flowing down from stones to stones and every plant life you can imagine growing amongst the waters! This water seemed to be coming from the Throne!

I zoomed out to get a bigger picture and there were rivers flowing out of the light up the mountain! There were rivers flowing out of the Throne! It all seemed to come straight from the Father Himself. I saw the rivers branch out and flow down past the walls, down into the forests, and then into what I can only describe as cities.

I looked and saw the first sight of reflected light. The river was very wide at this point and it seemed to be flowing directly into the middle of what was a city!

Then I instantly gathered my vision and looked all around and on the gentle slope down from the Father were cities and cities and more cities!

I had scriptures coming to me left and right!

> **Hebrews 11:16 (KJV)**
>
> **16 But now they desire a better country, that is, an heavenly: wherefore God is not ashamed to be called their God: for he hath prepared for them a city.**
>
> **Hebrews 12:22-23 (KJV)**
>
> **22 But ye are come unto mount Sion, and unto the city of the living God, the heavenly Jerusalem, and to an innumerable company of angels,**
>
> **23 To the general assembly and church of the firstborn, which are written in heaven, and to God the Judge of all, and to the spirits of just men made perfect,**
>
> **Philippians 3:20 (ESV)**
>
> **20 But our citizenship is in heaven, and from it we await a Savior, the Lord Jesus Christ,…**

There were so much light reflecting from these cities that I had to individually take effort to zoom into each one. I had to do this one at a time in order to see! Yes, I was able to do all of this in such a short time! The mind I had in Heaven would make Einstein and all the superheroes in Marvel movies look like babies!

I was aware that I was using what I believe is a glorified body, mind, eyes, etc. I was experiencing what we get to be like when we are in eternity with our glorified immortal body!

Philippians 3:21 (KJV)
> **²¹ Who shall change our vile body, that it may be fashioned like unto his glorious body…**

I took in the details of the first city. At first, I was taking it in as a small town like we would see in the country areas. It was surrounded by trees and it had a river flowing right down into the middle of the city. I then pierced inward to see what I wanted to see, and I had details flooding into my mind. I could sense that the river was at least a couple of miles wide going through the city. The roads were on both sides of the river and each of them were probably a mile wide each!

Psalm 46:4-5 (ESV)
> **⁴ There is a river whose streams make glad the city of God, the holy habitation of the Most High.**
> **⁵ God is in the midst of her; she shall not be moved;**

There was the most beautiful display of every kind of tree lining the river! I could see so many different trees flashing before my mind instantly. I was immediately understanding all the details of these trees: the fruit, leaves, heights, pleasure from eating them, etc. Oh my; this was already too much to take in!

Oh I was having so much insight flooding into me!

Psalm1:3 (KJV)
> **³ And he shall be <u>like a tree planted by the rivers of water</u>, that bringeth forth his fruit in his season; his leaf also shall not wither; and whatsoever he doeth shall prosper.**

Heaven Awaits Your Expression

Seriously! I was seeing some trees that had fruit that looked like diamonds!

Some leaves were what I will guess to be crystal, glass, or some kind of transparent see-through material. Oh, it was a sight to see. The trees were cascading over the river! These trees were eternity old! They were ancient trees who's branches went horizontally over the water! Some trees had roots that went into the water, came up out of the water, and had several trees grown up out of the root that surfaced! The trees themselves have intertwined themselves like a woven fabric all through the river!

The water was beautiful! There were people everywhere in the river! Believe this one- there were people in the trees! I mean, I could see kids up in the trees! It was like the trees were one of the greatest attractions for the kids to visit! Kids were everywhere! They were running on the branches that spanned across the river!

I saw some groups of kids racing across the river on these branches and laughing so loud! They were screaming in fun and running so fast! They were faster than jaguars in the Amazon! They were running and then OMG they ran and dove off a portion of the branches that were something like 100 ft or more above the river! They all dove off in a fun frenzy! Wait…that wasn't exactly diving!

They were flipping, gliding, spinning, and belly flopping, and straight up flying out over the water! These kids looked like what I remembered in a documentary on Netflix where all the birds dive into the water and go fishing! These kids all darted into the water so fast and effortlessly and that was it. They were gone!

I waited a moment to see them all come back to the water's surface, but they never came back. I was willing my mind to know more about the kids. I was really eager to know now!

I could feel the Spirit instantly inside of me bringing the knowing to my mind. The kids were under the water swimming and racing underneath as well. Do what!??? The kids could breathe underwater, swim, fly, and play underwater too? Wow!

Heaven Awaits Your Expression

These kids would play games all through the trees, in the sky, down underneath the water, and could never get hurt! That's just wonderful. Oh, I wished my kids could be playing with these kids!

I wanted deeply to see my own kids playing, singing, laughing, and chasing one another in this place. I resolved to make sure I was like Jesus and loving every kid I could. I knew Jesus was thinking of this place when He was blessing the little kids who came to him. He said, "For such is the kingdom of Heaven." (Mark 10:14)

These kids seemed to be free to be kids here! They seem to run and play, and all of the adults would celebrate them. They were cheered on by the bystanders. They were so loved. I could see angels and even humans all cheering for the kids. It seemed like there were fun games, sports if you will, for kids to do in Heaven. I didn't see anything that was what we experience here as organized sports, but I did see so many people involved with the kids.

It seemed that some folks who go to Heaven enjoy spending an eternity blessing these kids. Are they all citizens who stop and take pleasure in watching the kids play? It was becoming more apparent. The angels were kind of like supervisors, teachers, and coaches to the kids.

It dawned on me that these kids seemed to be in their schooling! This was education in Heaven! The kids had teachers from other glorified believers, the angels, and Jesus Himself. All of this was becoming more and more apparent as I watched.

Then the Spirit gave me another insight, "These are their parents, teachers, and others who give their talent for all eternity to the knowledge of the kids before you."

Oh, the sweet kindness of the Lord. I was only here for what seemed like minutes and I've seen the most BEAUTIFUL kindness of our Lord to the kids of Heaven. I was now staring at the parents. Those were the parents of the kids. No wonder they were cheering with glory and joy as they watched their little ones running, diving, swimming, and jumping with joy with the other kids. The kids got to experience everything they learned about.

They learned up in the trees, in the clouds, in the water, on the mountains, and by each monument in Heaven.

Oh, the beauty of God's design for the young lives of children! Oh, that's how I wish I learned! I
 wish I could've been running around in the mountains of TN and learning how to subtract, add, and multiply! I would've been much happier doing that than sitting in a caged desk, in a caged room, in a caged building, and listening to a hireling teach me.

Here, the parents, the angels, and Jesus Himself were all involved with educating the kids! I want my kids to be raised here! I thought about the parents. What is it about the parents? They got to assist in educating their kids! One thing I learned- education never stops in Heaven. It seemed everyone learned for eternity. Everyone would continue discovering amazing knowledge forever!

I remembered His Words in scripture.

Isaiah 54:13 (KJV)
[13] And all thy children shall be taught of the Lord; and great shall be the peace of thy children.

The Lord began to take my attention away and towards the mighty plazas on both sides of the rivers. It looks like roads on both sides of the river. Likewise, at the same time, it seemed to be more like plazas. It was like the area before great buildings on the Earth.

I thought of the Pope at the Vatican. There's nothing but a large plaza lining both sides of the river and the park area where the trees are.

There was a large river flowing down through the city. On both sides of the river were the most beautiful trees and landscaping. It was filled with fruit trees, bushes, flowers, grass, large gems, diamonds, and stones I've never had the challenge of describing. Some stones seemed like a live stone being that shined colorful lights in all directions. The lights were in reaction to all that looked at it. You would look at the stone and it would give you a color show. It was beyond my words.

Heaven Awaits Your Expression

People were walking throughout the landscaping and walking on the water, and swimming in the water, and sitting on the branches of the trees.

To the edge of the park landscaping were golden edges that lined the plaza roads. The roads were constructed with what looked like a mile of multicolored stone. The edges of the plaza road had what seemed to be high towers or columns.

These tower columns lined up and down the banks of the rivers in the areas where the trees were scarce. It seemed like the trees gave way to each tower. The branches of the trees knew not to grow toward these towers! The towers were perfectly lined up down the long roads of the city on both sides of the river.

These marble and gold looking columns looked like stages or balconies that stoop up high overlooking the streets. There were people on top of the columns on the stage/balcony area. They spoke out in loud thundering voices publishing the praises of the Lord. These people seemed to be proclaiming the good works of the Father and Jesus. I started to pick up on what one was saying!

He thundered out, "Our Heavenly Father has moved upon the children in Haiti and we have received many into the fold. We have had missionaries there for only two months and we have had over 133 souls repent! Our precious Spirit has drawn many more believers into deep passionate prayer for their land!

Many more are being obedient to our wonderful Commission and are speaking out the praises and Good News of Jesus Christ! We are seeing the Kingdom of our God advance in the land!"

The crowd that was below and all throughout that quarter of the city seemed to all with one voice respond in shouting and rejoicing and many volumes of worship went up to the Lord!

How did I know it was the whole quarter of the city? I am not sure. What I can tell you is, I could see light coming up from that whole section. It seemed that when they would bless the Lord, light would shine bright around them!

Heaven Awaits Your Expression

Another wonderful detail that came to my mind was how that I knew people were in their own mansions/buildings/homes and they heard the man's proclamations!

Everyone responded in kind to the news. So, I guess you can hear the news of the work on Earth from your mansions. You are kept up to speed about what's happening on Earth at all times. WOW

The Lord shared some scriptures inside of me:

Isaiah: 52:7-9

> **7 How beautiful upon the mountains are the feet of him that bringeth good tidings, that publisheth peace; that bringeth good tidings of good, that publisheth salvation; that saith unto Zion, Thy God reigneth!**
>
> **8 Thy watchmen shall lift up the voice; with the voice together shall they sing: for they shall see eye to eye, when the Lord shall bring again Zion.**
>
> **9 Break forth into joy, sing together, ye waste places of Jerusalem: for the Lord hath comforted his people, he hath redeemed Jerusalem.**

The Lord showed me that these people stand up and publish good tidings, publish peace, bring about news of the good that happens on Earth because of the Lord, publishes the salvation of sinners, and declares glorious praises to the people of Zion.

They give the people in Heaven constant news that bring about praises, honor, and glory to The Father!

How beautiful is that! How amazing to know that you will hear the latest news on the Earth. You get to hear news pertaining to the areas in which you labored when you were on the Earth. You can still watch over the promises the Father gave you on the Earth. You can still receive the answers to prayer even after you have gone to glory. When a prayer was answered, you would know!

People praised God within the crowd. I knew instantly that these folks had loved ones that were born again within that news just proclaimed. People were seeing promises from God fulfilled just then!

How amazing!

I remembered the passage in Hebrews 11 talking about those who were listed as examples of faith on the Earth.

Hebrews 11:13

> **¹³ These all died in faith, not having received the promises, but having seen them afar off, and were persuaded of them, and embraced them, and confessed that they were strangers and pilgrims on the earth.**

These believers died without having received their promise! They still obtain their promises even after they pass away! They are the great cloud of witnesses watching the race continue on the Earth.

I looked then at the buildings and the towers. I still don't know what all these buildings were. I think I knew in that moment, but some details escape me. Perhaps I'm not supposed to remember?

I saw what I knew to be homes! This must've been the mansions I heard Jesus speak of in John 14!

John 14:1-3 (KJV)

> **¹ Let not your heart be troubled: ye believe in God, believe also in me.**
>
> **² <u>In my Father's house are many mansions</u>: if it were not so, I would have told you. I go to prepare a place for you.**
>
> **³ And if I go and prepare a place for you, I will come again, and receive you unto myself; that where I am, there ye may be also.**

I saw some mansions that were on their very own lot, some were like condos, some like townhouses, and some were like the row houses you see in big cities.

Heaven Awaits Your Expression

I looked out towards the outskirts of the city area and I saw house after house! These were all surrounded by trees and different monuments. Some houses were several stories high!

Some were long, short, and even on air. I didn't have time to study the details of each and every one I saw unfortunately.

I saw some glass houses that looked a lot like federal buildings in DC. It seemed to be a house though.

WOW, that's large. I saw some that looked like the White House with the white stone. But this stone was ONE SLAB OF STONE and it wasn't just white. It had veins of glorious color inside of it. It looked like some had precious blue-ish topaz marbled all throughout the slabs.

Some had gold, and some had what I can only describe as a flame design within the stone. Picture a flame in your mind. You see the bottom has hues of blue, purple, and then invisible, then orange, reds, yellows, and bright colors only a fire can give. That's exactly how some stonework look like on these houses. Some literally looked like it was a large flame of Gold. It was transparent at some portions.

Literally, it was see-through stone in some areas. It was somewhat like the Epoxy resin chemical you pour onto counter tops or tables to make a glass like veneer. Just beautiful and not suitable for me to use the English language.

One mansion looked like solid glass, one looked like see through water, and one looked like all gold.

Some buildings I could tell were public buildings that stood very high. I think perhaps these were libraries, schools, and places of worship.

What I did see along the streets and the open areas within this particular city was what looked like memorials and statues that told stories of men and women of God on the Earth that did many acts to give God glory! I wish I could've seen who those were for!

I know one thought that stuck within my spirit after that discovery. I decided in my heart that I wanted to be a man on the Earth worthy of a Memorial here. Would God see fit to tell the citizens of Heaven what He accomplishes through me?

I wanted to be one of the saints honored to have a memorial in Heaven! I remembered Acts 10 where it said that Cornelius had a memorial in Heaven because of the alms he did! Perhaps that's what those were?

Acts 10: 1-4

1 There was a certain man in Caesarea called Cornelius, a centurion of the band called the Italian band,

2 A devout man, and one that feared God with all his house, which gave much alms to the people, and prayed to God alway.

3 He saw in a vision evidently about the ninth hour of the day an angel of God coming in to him, and saying unto him, Cornelius.

4 And when he looked on him, he was afraid, and said, What is it, Lord? And he said unto him, Thy prayers and thine alms are come up for <u>a memorial before God.</u>

I determined to one day visit each and every one of the memorials and hear for myself what humans have accomplished on the Earth for Jesus. I felt so encouraged to see that! I had a powerful urge to see what was POSSIBLE for me as a human! I felt like I could do ANYTHING I knew another could do! The same Spirit was in me! Oh, how enthusiastic I felt as I saw these monuments and memorials! I knew Jesus was feeling praised as believers and kids would come up and see the feats these men and women accomplished on the Earth!

Wait! How could they see? Oh, I wanted to know! I think they could go up to a memorial and see videos and replays of the miracles, salvations, and battles won for the Lord! It seemed as though the men or women being memorialized were actually standing nearby the statues to tell firsthand what the Lord did through them. WOW!!!

I was thinking a million thoughts at the same time! Oh, how wonderful!

I knew I must move on. I took in the view of the city once again.

Heaven Awaits Your Expression

The amazing part of the buildings were how the light reflected off of them! It was amazing to see how light was everywhere! There were stars in the sky reflecting! The buildings reflected light! The streets reflected light. Even the water and the trees!

The streets were pure gold, some were pure diamond, some were pure emerald green, and some were pink ruby like colors! All of those streets reflected light brilliantly with their particular colors adding to the aurora! This all reminded me of the Northern Lights.

It's fascinating how all the people were used to all the bright light! I sure wasn't used to it yet!

Light was everywhere!

Then, I remembered the light reflecting on the water behind me. This whole time, I was standing in the exact same spot by the pool of water with Jesus on my right side, and the cities of Heaven before me! I stopped, paused, and wondered. The Father is over there! I gathered my bearings and mentally placed God the Father back behind me as I turned to the water. Like a kid learning a new word, or tasting a new taste, or discovering something for the very first time, I realized that the light was reflecting toward me. Wow! I thought about our natural Earth physics or physical laws. According to physics, or at least all of my Earthly experiences, the light should be reflecting in that direction! I pointed in the opposite direction of where the Father's bright supernova star bright light was coming from.

I thought in the direction on the other side of the water. God is behind me, and His light is beaming like crazy in this direction! It should be reflecting the other direction! Whoa…how does it do that?

Jesus was in my thoughts. He could hear me taking in all the discoveries! I was entranced. I was in complete awe of His presence with me and at the same time I was just jaw dropped at the surroundings. I don't know how I could do both…but I could. On Earth, I can't do two things at one time. Ask my wife. She has to get my attention "fully" before she says something. It's funny…sometimes!

Heaven Awaits Your Expression

Jesus was not really speaking but sharing his emotion with me. I knew He was taking great pleasure in everything I was taking in through my eyes and all my fresh new senses. He was present with me AND IN ME. That was an experience in itself. His person beside me was registering with every single particle of my being.

I felt alive from head to toe. I felt alive inside of me. Like even my different parts of my body all had a voice in the matter. All of me knew. All of me could hear Jesus emanating a message that He loved me. He was love. I was standing beside Love. There's no other love. He is the rarest, the only one…the rarest of rare.

He was the only Love you could find. There was no other love out there. It was like finding the one rarest of gems, emerald, gold, etc. It was like finding the rarest of elements in the universe. So rare, that there was only one to find! It was Him. He was that! He was. He is. What He is, He is.

I had names of God rushing throughout my memory banks. I sifted through names on Earth we call Him by, like, "I AM THAT I AM" and that one was the one that stood with me the most. I thought "He is that He is." When I think of Love. He is Love. He is so much love! He is the epitome of what my current revelation of His love is. He…IS…more than what my discovery of what He is…IS. Oh, my words are not working for this!

He just regarded me like I was His kid…his young son. I was loved like a young baby son. At the same time, I was talked to like I was fully mature. He loved me like you love your newborn baby, or your toddler taking their first step, their first smile, or their first word! Oh, He was looking all the way through me. I knew instantly that because I'm one of the Father's sons, He did everything He did for me! He loved me, and loves me, and will love me all in the same revelation. Upon each heartbeat…that is what I was taking in from Him.

He was asking me if I was delighting in what I see? Yet, He never said a word from His mouth!

Jesus was sounding out inside my being. He was a part of each of my experiences, to the most minute detail. He was giving a kind of approval that, in that moment, I realized I was created for. I felt worthwhile. I felt accepted. It was the only approval I've ever felt was completely real. It made all of my human interactions with important people seem so fake. It just made me realize that all I strived for in my past was vanity and not full. It was only in part.

The Wholeness of this split second with Jesus made me realize I was made, I was built, and I was designed to interact with Jesus! It was my purpose!

CHAPTER 2

EYES LIKE STARS

"His eyes are such a torch, such a burning star, a sun so deep and holy, that it can take on the radiating colors and expressions of His creation depending on the Beholder.."

My goodness, I was filled with love for Jesus! I felt like I could barely hold myself together. I was going to explode with praise and tears and worship! It was swelling up from out of my belly. The scripture came to mind instantly of the "fountain of living water in my belly welling up into eternal life" as Jesus spoke of in John 4. He said it was a fountain- a well. Oh, I instantly wanted to ask Jesus to tell those on Earth that those geysers in Yellowstone seemed to be more like what it's like!

I thought back to the Earthly moments in my past, where I experienced intercessory prayer. I was thinking of the deep overwhelming burden, or urgent desire bursting up inside of me to go to God in prayer. I remember a "travail" that came on me the day before my brother decided to follow me into Salvation. I was a teenager. I remembered that one above all the others. That was the constant feeling I've had the WHOLE TIME being near Jesus. This emotion I feel now is wonderful! It's very moving, like I MUST respond to Him in worship! I must bless His name!

Heaven Awaits Your Expression

I turned to release a praise. Maybe a worship? Oh, I wanted to give...no release... some kind of shout, or something!

I could explode! I felt like I wasn't even worthy to be here. I wasn't even sure how I felt.

But I knew I was going to give my most authentic "ALL" in adoration. How that would look? I have no idea. It was my first time standing in the presence of Jesus side by side! I stopped caring about how I was supposed to do it and decided to yield to the gentleness inside me. I thought I should just stop letting my thoughts go in a million directions and yield to Him. He's standing right there.

"Come on Brock. Focus. You are with Jesus!" I poised myself.

I was in the effort of turning and I heard myself saying loudly, "My eyes can see all this color! My eyes can see! Oh, it's wonderful! It's beautiful! I'm so excited to see! My eyes! My eyes have been opened!"

Instead of making it all the way around to Jesus, my eyes stopped on a man. A tall man. He was slender, tall, and had an educated aura about him. I knew instantly that from his countenance, he was one who knew everything he needed to know. He was one who kept a record. He had eyes. I was locked in on his eyes! Intelligence. Keen and Skillful Wisdom were thoughts in my mind. His other features seemed to be in a dimness. I could make out that he had golden curly hair. Short, curly hair that seemed to be gold from an ancient most holy artifact. Wow. His hair is golden!

His complexion was what came to my mind's eye, the light purple hue that I have seen on some Mango fruit. Yeah. Mangos is what I thought. It wasn't an Earthly purple! It was a Heavenly kind of purple that we don't have here! I don't know how to describe his complexion...but it was similar to the gold and purple that mix on some fresh Mangos! Oh, who knows what the color is called in Heaven. Maybe they wouldn't even call it purple?

I have seen freshly ripened Mangos from Colombia and there is a moment...a split amount of time I'm sure...that you can see the Heavenly tone of this angel's skin between the gold and the purple on a Mango.

It is clear. There are colors in Heaven that we don't have. Or do we?

Heaven Awaits Your Expression

It seems from this experience that perhaps we DO have the colors here on Earth.

It's just that our death-stained eyes are stripped of the retina capabilities to see the refection of the full number of colors that really are before us. We have lost a spectrum of the God given color palette we are to be able to see! Something is missing within our Earthly eyes!

Right then, I sensed the inner working of Jesus and His Spirit moving memories around within me! I had the faintest of quick memories come to my mind.

A long time ago, I had seen a rainbow once on a beautiful rainy afternoon. I took a picture of it on Earth. (Mind you...on Earth, I would never have remembered this). Was this memory stored somewhere else? Was this memory in me? Was it coming from me...or from the Lord? Here, it seemed that both were the same! And yes, this is crazy! I am able to think multiple thoughts and process many things ALL AT ONCE! That's something I can't do on Earth. It's like a strong processor in a computer at home. I can multitask like I've never been able to EVER.

Back to the rainbow memory. I took a picture of a beautiful rainbow on a rainy day. It was a gorgeous and huge rainbow. I remember it being the largest and closest rainbow I've ever seen! It seemed to be coming up from the Earth somewhere near me!

What seemed to stick with the memory was how the rainbow had all the typical rainbow colors on the bows as you would see on any rainbow. But this rainbow had two or three of each of the colors. It was like it had double or triple the bows as they usually do. I was up close...and it seemed that perhaps all rainbows are like that if you are up close!

Then it hit me...inside.

It was like the Spirit highlighted this moment.

I thought to myself, "Perhaps each rainbow truly does have more colors than what we typically define with our Earthly eyes! Maybe there are more primary colors!?"

Oh, the mystery behind these wonderful colors!

The Lord flooded me with scripture references. I was shown multiple examples in the Bible where men had experienced visions of Heaven, of angels, of Jesus, of the Throne, and mentioned the colors they saw. They would say things like, "the color <u>of</u> amber, or <u>like</u> the color of Emerald" or "<u>like</u> an emerald rainbow." It was revealed to me then and it was understood as these scriptures came into me instantly.

These men did their best to describe the colors they saw with the closest Earthly description they could use to articulate what they were seeing!

I will list some of the scriptures here:

Ezekiel 1:26-28 (KJV- The prophet Ezekiel's vision)

26 And above the firmament that was over their heads was the *likeness* of a throne, *as the appearance of* a sapphire stone: and upon *the likeness of* the throne was the *likeness as the appearance of* a man above upon it.

27 And I saw *as the color of* amber, *as the appearance of* fire round about within it, from the appearance of his loins even upward, and from the appearance of his loins even downward, I saw *as it were the appearance of* fire, and it had brightness round about.

28 As the appearance of the bow that is in the cloud in the day of rain (rainbow), so was the appearance of the brightness round about. This was the appearance of the likeness of the glory of the Lord. And when I saw it, I fell upon my face, and I heard a voice of one that spake.

Daniel 10:5-6 (KJV- The prophet Daniel's vision)

5 Then I lifted up mine eyes, and looked, and behold a certain man clothed in linen, whose loins were girded with fine gold of Uphaz:

> **6** His body also was like the beryl, and his face as the appearance of lightning, and his eyes as lamps of fire, and his arms and his feet like in color to polished brass, and the voice of his words like the voice of a multitude.

> **Revelation 4:2-4 (KJV- The Apostle John's vision)**
> **2** And immediately I was in the spirit: and, behold, a throne was set in Heaven, and one sat on the throne.
> **3** And he that sat *was to look upon like a* jasper and a sardine stone: and there was a rainbow round about the throne, *in sight like unto an* emerald.

These colors were fascinating. I will share more as we go. But one thing is for sure. Trying to describe what I see, is the challenge. The best I can do is rely upon the Lord and give the best descriptions I can. I mean, think back in the ancient days, when Ezekiel was trying to describe the Throne of God. He didn't have any knowledge of what a supernova, nebula, or galaxy even looked like! They didn't have NASA back then. There was no quick Google Search or YouTube! These guys did their very best to describe what they saw! It's tough!

It made me think of the Apostle Paul.

> **2 Cor 12:1-4 (KJV)**
> [1] ...I will come to visions and revelations of the Lord.
> [2] I knew a man in Christ above fourteen years ago, (whether in the body, I cannot tell; or whether out of the body, I cannot tell: God knoweth;) such an one caught up to the third heaven.
> [3] And I knew such a man, (whether in the body, or out of the body, I cannot tell: God knoweth;)
> [4] How that he was caught up into paradise, and <u>heard unspeakable words</u>, which it is not lawful for a man to utter.

Heaven Awaits Your Expression

Even the Apostle Paul found it hard to describe what he saw when he had visions. He himself experienced what I was seeing.

Back to the angel. I was taking in all these details. Remember, these details are literally coming to me and processing through me faster than what we call a "split second." More like a nanosecond. I'm just trying to record as much of my thoughts here as I possibly can for my readers. Please Lord, help me.

I was taking in the features of the tall slender angel with golden hair and I could not get my eyes off of his eyes! I was supposed to look at his eyes- I knew it.

He said to me, "Look into my eyes" and he stepped with one step what would've taken me several steps! He stepped right to me, his face in front of my face. The vibrations coming off his being were like hums of life. I could feel him without touching him! I could hear his life in him. Wow. I was looking into his eyes. Blue.

I could see blue. His eyes were a "like a" blue light. It was breathtaking! I was looking at what I can only explain as a blue birthing star. A blue nebula of radiant dazzling history. I was looking at the history, no, the revelation, no, the time, or maybe the depth of his being? It looked like a blue nebula star with a perfect pattern of radial design that was its own brilliant star or stars. His eyes had its own star, with star dust, with light, radiance, depth, and color! There were so many blues within that blue! Oh my! Just fascinating!

I have never ever looked into a man's eyes on Earth like this! I would never! I mean, let's be real, guys don't do that where I'm from. Well, I think some may. Some love rainbows! This was different! This was an experience! I could look into this angel's eyes and see something of a creation story.

I could see he was birthed as a light star (words fail me) and through millennia he has learned of our Heavenly Father, seen many exploits, beheld greatness, taken in his own wonder of God, his own revelations and discoveries of the Love of God like I have! He's just had all of eternity to behold His Majesty!

Heaven Awaits Your Expression

His eyes told me that he's had ancient revelations of my Heavenly Father and yet, he doesn't feel like he's scratched the surface. He has only briefly gazed upon the Holy One!

He was looking into my eyes and I perceived that he could see into me as well! He was probably not getting much. I thought to myself with a small giggle. I am like 33 years of ancient flesh and bone. I've now seen my first few glimpses of Heavenly realities! There won't be much for him to see.

I took this all in. I was in a state of awareness of myself as I never have been. I just saw my very first angel and I'm feeling aware of myself? What in the world is this? He is way taller than me, probably 8 ft or 9 ft. I'm not quite sure with this fellow…the rest of his body was in a slight dim still. I was only seeing what seemed how much I was allowed to see. Not sure.

But I thought I'd be awestruck at seeing an angel. And wait, I wasn't on my face as one dead! Every story I read of angels coming in the Bible had the people falling as dead men. They were frightened!

In this setting, I believe it was because Jesus was with me. Maybe it's not like that in Heaven? Maybe in Heaven, I only bow and fall down as one dead before Jesus? It's still fascinating to me how I thought about so much detail in Heaven. I'm doing my best to remember it all.

I had a knowing that I was supposed to be finished with the moment looking into the angel's eyes and turn around. So, I did as instructed.

I turned and saw Jesus. This time I knew I could take in more of Him. Not all of Him was fully available in light for me to see. I was seeing His hair. I looked. It was brown. It was brown, wavy, and shiny and healthy looking. Well, it looked human!

I was thinking that, and Jesus said to me, "I keep my hair as it was on Earth, for those to see how much I love them".

I cried. I lost it. I can't remember much of that moment. It seemed I was lost somewhere that only happens when you die a death. It was what I can explain as the very moment I took on another expression?

I don't know. But the revelation of that moment made me transform into a whole new being. It was like a metamorphic moment. I cried.

I lost my old self and came out of the moment as a new person. It was my first experience in Heaven where the revelation coming from the Lord changed me. It's not much in light of eternity. But inside me...I became new. Wow.

I don't know how long I cried. Look. I cried. Oh, I cried. It was beautiful soul deep crying. Oh, how He loved me! How he thought of little Ole Me! I am just one human, on a planet full of humans, animals, birds, fish, etc. He knows all by name. He knows the number of hairs on my head. I remembered then; He even calls all the stars by name.

Psalm 147:4 (KJV)
⁴ He telleth the number of the stars; he <u>calleth them all by their names.</u>

I remembered some random piece of knowledge from something I heard back in my Earthly history. I remembered that there were hundreds of billions of stars! How did He know all their names? If they had names, then they too were a part of His created order! They too were particles that were alive and made by Him and carried the same God light within each atom like I did! Oh, the depth of revelation from every single moment with Jesus! I don't even know how long I've been here with Him and I can't remember already the depth of Knowledge I've learned about him in just a short moment. I cried some more.

Psalm 84:11
¹¹ For the Lord God is a <u>sun</u> and shield:

I remembered the reference in James 1:17 calling Him the "Father of Lights," the "morning star" in Rev. 2:28, and the "bright morning star" in Rev. 22:16.

I cried because I was so dependent on Him. I cried because I have not been perfect. I have not been fully obedient. I know so much of His word.

I have laid hands on and healed the sick, cast out devils, cleansed a leper, tried to raise a dead guy once and I didn't succeed.

Heaven Awaits Your Expression

I have won many to Jesus and seen so many amazing things with God! I've seen so much demonstration of God's power. I've been so close to the things of God. I've hungered for His word on and off my whole life it seems. I've been close to Him and then conveniently turned my eyes from the needs of hurting people around me. I've thought of myself. I cried. I cried because of my selfish ways. I was sick to think how I owed debt, how I paid bills past due, how I had not treated another human right, how I acted selfishly, and sinned against this loving Jesus before me. I cried because I would rather be HERE for two minutes and truly know God rather than spend 18 years of my born-again life wading in cesspools of religious Christianity. I could've just sought Him with my whole heart and found a moment to be at His feet. I could've traded it all...I mean all of my life...all of me...to just have this moment with Jesus! It was an encounter with Grace.

I saw, felt, smelled, tasted, and heard LOVE from my Beloved Jesus! I could sense Him fully from every piece of me! I opened my eyes even more! I realized that I didn't even have my contacts in at all. Oh, silly me...I don't need my contacts or glasses here! There I go again thinking with my Earthly mind. Ugh.

And wait! I could smell! On Earth, my nose didn't work too well! I had a natural thick mucus or sinus that kept me from smelling well...but NOW I could smell really well! Heck, I could even identify the smells! I had some kind of knowledge about what ever single smell was around me.

It was very odd, the smells themselves told you where they came from! How do you explain that?

Jesus had his normal Judean brown hair that was somewhat past ear length. Between ear and shoulder neck length...then all my words stopped. I had remembered the girl who painted a portrait of Jesus. She had it right! I made a note to myself to go look that picture up later and see how close she got it.

~

As soon as I was finished with this vision, I started to search online for many different things. One thing I searched for, was the artist named Akiane Kramarik.

Heaven Awaits Your Expression

Her painting of Jesus called the Prince of Peace was so right on, it made me cry as soon as it came up on the Google search! If you want to know what Jesus looks like, then look up her painting. The one thing I'll point out though...Jesus is now in Heaven and He is in a glorified body. You can look at Him over and over and over and never really take in all the details. His eyes, for example, were different tones of colors each time I saw them. In His Earthly state, they were (mainly) one color and then when I was worshiping Him, I saw them as the sun in our galaxy. At other times they were like flames, like a star burning, and so forth.

He is God Almighty. You don't get Him figured out. You don't get just one image of Him and you have Him. Oh no. You will never see ALL of Him that you will want to. You will behold Him for all of eternity. Each time you see Him you will leave a new person yourself and have a deep urge inside you to come back and behold Him again! Each time you experience Him, you have seen Him like it's the first time. God is not one to become common. He is holy. He is the only one of His kind. There's nothing rarer in all Creation...than the one who did the creating. His name is Jesus!

~

OK, back to seeing Jesus!

I let my mind think of so much more In Jesus. He was declaring me inside of Him. I don't know how to describe that well either. He was, from within His being, radiating from His heart to mine, who I am because of Him! Oh I cried. I'm telling you I cried with joy. I was feeling overwhelmed with love, joy, peace...just happy crying.

I knew that Jesus looked exactly like the portrait of the Akiane girl. I think she was from Ukraine or something like that. But she was right! That picture is right on! I was amazed at His eyes!

His eyes. He said to me within my mind, "Come, look at MY eyes". I was instantly before Him and eye to eye. I don't know how I stood there. Everything within me was falling to the ground like I weighed nothing.

I can't remember if I was floating, or perhaps the angels were holding me up. Maybe Jesus held me there with his power? Who knows! I just know I was looking into the eyes of Jesus! Oh, the eyes!

"His eyes were like a flame of fire." That scripture came immediately to my mind. But it's one thing to read that phrase and picture what they look like within your mind and it's another thing to be up close and having Jesus command you to look into His eyes. I was not only face to face with Him, but my vision. My eyes…my whole vision went fully INTO HIS ONE EYE. I was beholding what seemed like a sun! It was a sun in all its brilliance. I knew that He could pulverize me with the brightness and even the energy from the sun within his eye. His eye was a star bright supernova of pure Gold like cloud, strands of light and color. He had it all in there. So much to take in. He has the eyes of all eyes. He has an eye that tells ALL. His eye was unending. When I say unending, I mean, beyond the darkness of what we call ever expanding light from our expanding universes. Beyond the ever-expanding light is what we as humans can only describe as darkness. The light has to reflect on something for us to see, right? Well, from within the Eyes of Immanuel Himself, the Son of the Living God was beholding all things from His eyes.

In His eyes were stars, stars birthing, universes, people, races, beings, animals, every type of creature and life lighted being in all His created order. It was beyond me. No other way to describe this but, His eyes were everything. I could see what seemed to be a star nebula radiating color in the likeness of a galaxy.

> **Job 41:18 (ESV)**
> [11] …**and His eyes are like the eyelids of the dawn**
> **Hebrews 4:13 (ESV)**
> [13] **And no creature is hidden from his sight, but all are naked and exposed to the eyes of him to whom we must give account.**

Heaven Awaits Your Expression

    Oh, I am not even sure if I was seeing His eyes as they are normally? Is this His normal eyes or is He wanting me to see something through His eyes?
    Is it possible His eyes are such a torch, such a burning star, a sun so deep and holy, that it can take on the radiating colors and expressions of His creation depending on the Beholder? Perhaps His eyes were showing me what I needed to see? I am just silent.
    My eyes are taking in too much knowledge. My eyes seemed to be taking pictures. My Eyes seemed to be trying to take video. I don't think the frames at which my mind was gathering the moving images before me in His eyes were suitable for the moment. I felt like a movie producer or director. I wanted a slow-motion scene that caught a 360 panoramic detail filled capture of the scene before me.
    I was thinking of the Matrix when they first started that technology. They had all those cameras set up all over a whole scene from every single angle filming all at once JUST to catch one scene in slow motion! I felt like the director of the Matrix, and I wanted to film that scene. I felt like I was present, and the scene was happening, but I had the wrong equipment to capture every detail I needed to record!
    Oh, I wanted all of the detail. I saw many galaxies. I saw what I will go out on a limb and say that some knowledge within His eyes were veiled for me to comprehend. I wondered if there was other life on the other planets/universes He was mindful of? Were they also within His eyes? Then, perhaps maybe, there could be another alien race who is worshipping the same Almighty Holy Big God I'm experiencing. Maybe I'll get to ask Him that at some point?
    Well, at this point, I couldn't take any more. Jesus knowing my mind's thoughts, brought me back to the golden pathway. I knew I was on it because I looked back down to gather my bearings again.
    I saw that I didn't have any shoes on! I was barefoot! Oh, the gold felt so good. It seemed that because I was looking at the gold, it knew I was, and little ripples of vibration went out from my feet.

Energy was placed within my body through my feet. It was impressive. This gold was actively alive. Interesting.

I wanted to think more, but I was just looking into the eyes of Jesus! I assumed my same amazed silent pale faced fear of God posture that seemed to have me stiff as a board.

My mouth seemed to work. I said, "Jesus, your eyes... and his eyes (pointing at the scribe angel), are like stars! They are so wonderful!"

Jesus, as if He had this planned, looked up. I knew I was to follow Him instinctively. So, I looked up, and there were a lot of stars in the beautiful sky!

I looked up and said, "Wow, those stars are so beautiful! Look at the colors! Stars on Earth are nowhere close to these! Stars at home all kind of look the same to the naked eye!"

Jesus, with one motion, said to another angel standing to my left, "Bring me that star. That one!" Jesus pointed.

I was like, "Whaaaaat? You can go grab a star? Whaaaaa!!! Holy Moly!"

Another thing that had me keeping myself contained was the fact that I forgot about the 2nd being waiting for me on the other side of the pool of water.

I turned to see who the Lord was talking to. All I saw was a golden dash. He was off with what I knew was a slowed speed. The angel gracefully darted toward the star. I knew inside of me that he was way faster than that. But it was obvious that he was doing this on purpose. Or...was he really truly traveling at the speed of thought? Was I able to see speed differently here? Were my new eyes that different? Oh I'm tripping now! You have got to be kidding. I don't even know if my mind is completely different or is he being nice and going slow?

I knew Jesus was listening and I became silent. I was kind of embarrassed. As I was kicking myself inwardly and thinking to myself, "It really doesn't matter does it? Your standing with Jesus and that's an angel! Stop getting distracted on the details and focus on Jesus! He's right here beside you and look at what's fully happening in front of your eyes!"

Heaven Awaits Your Expression

Then I know I must've blushed. Jesus was looking at me and humored. LOL...yeah, I laughed out loud. Jesus smiled and gave me an approving look...that look only a parent knows. I heard Him think to me, "Brock, take in every detail you can. You are here to take it all in. Oh, and is the angel going at the speed of thought? Yes. Is the angel going gracefully so that you can see him?

Yes. It's both. He's your angel. He serves Me day and night. He serves Me in his service to you. He is serving Me and loving Me by retrieving the star. He's loving you by letting you see the full assignment unfold before your own eyes. He's of the same service like unto you. He lives to please Me. The greatest of intentions that please Me are to Love Me...and serve Me with all of your heart, mind, soul, and strength. The second is to love Me as you love your neighbor..."

I had an immediate thought within myself. It wasn't even a full thought. But as soon as I began to think it, He answered me.

I thought of the scripture where Jesus said to love others as He has loved us. Right then, Jesus continued without missing a beat.

"BUT as you are just thinking correctly, I replaced that with the law of freedom, and that is to Love others as I have loved you. Your angel does the same. It pleases Me when He loves Me with excellent service. It pleases Me when He loves you and the others here within My Holy Kingdom. He's coming back with this star. I want you to look up close to this star."

The angel proudly and amazingly with so much grace landed strongly to the surface of God beside Jesus. I noticed the vibrations from the Gold upon his impact. It wasn't much different from each step of mine! Hmmm...no answer in my brain explains how the physics are working here. Perhaps he was slowing down and landing so gracefully because that's what you do before Jesus?

He stood there and I couldn't take in the features of the angel yet. All I could see was the star. This star was brought down to me, handed to me at chest level. I did take in the fact that this angel had to be like 14-16 feet tall.

Heaven Awaits Your Expression

Ok, maybe 14. Geez, I didn't have time to measure the big guy! I just saw a glimmer of God…and the bright shining star.

The star was surprisingly small. It was placed within my hold at the size of a 2-3 feet wide exercise ball. It was like the one my wife used during pregnancy. That was my only recollection of the size. It was white in color primarily. It had the same look of a nebula star! It wasn't even a white color. Something brighter. It was like the bright blinding white that comes from a welder's torch.

They have to wear a face mask/eye protection that keeps them from being blinded by the light. Hey, now that I think about it, my eyes didn't need goggles or glasses in Heaven! I just absorbed an un-human spectrum of light that I could never take in back in the States! This was peculiar. It was fascinating that my eyes seem to be able to switch from light reception to infrared. On Earth, I could focus my eyes in on one object or focus my pupils in and out depending on the amount of light was coming at me. These Heavenly eyes were able to adjust more than what our latest greatest digital cameras do. Oh, my goodness how spectacular!

I was holding the star by the nucleus at the core. The light was swirling around with a rotating star system around the inner star. Oh, I was literally freaking out with this. The star was built like the eyes of Jesus and the eyes of the angel! The stars were a galaxy within themselves.

I remembered then a deep piece of memory about the study I did on cells, atoms, and all this retrieval from biology class (or from somewhere). I was seeing how the smallest of atoms were created as little universe/galaxy systems almost. The smallest of God's creations were even created like the makeup of this star! The knowledge of the smallest of our quantum physics was brought back to me. I read a book one time describing what it was like to use a quantum microscope to see the quantum physics of a living cell. They can see the smallest of what the invisible biology of life on Earth is. That is the smallest we know. At that size, it's also a galaxy like phenomenon. Particles orbit the atoms/nucleus, etc. I was having remembrances of things I studied a long time ago.

But, was it a long time ago? In Heaven it didn't even seem like yesterday. Oh wow! Time is different here...oh this is taking me over the edge! I'm in Heaven!

Jesus was whispering to me, "Brock, everything I've created has my stamp of approval! Everything is a copy from out of my Father. As I took the rib from Adam and created every human being, so have I taken of my light, the same light you see in My eyes, and in your eyes, and in this star and placed it in every living being within the order of all

My creation. Every star that you see in space is many multitudes of smaller atom sized stars. Brock, you are not insignificant in any way to Me. I am in You and you are in Me. Anyone who is in ME, is honored by My Father and Myself. You have what a star has within both of your eyes.

The power that holds every atom together within every star, within every atom of created particles, and the very power that makes up My being...is living within you. My Spirit is Me. We are Spirit and those who worship Us are spirit. When I recreate you at your new birth, when My Spirit becomes one with you...you are totally new. Brock, you are Me and you. You are Me on Earth, and I am you here. We are united in a Heavenly defined unity."

I was having these verses in my mind as He was speaking.

1 John 4:17 (KJV)

> **Herein is our love made perfect, that we may have boldness in the day of judgment: because <u>as he is, so are we in this world.</u>**

Galatians 2:20 (KJV)

> **I am crucified with Christ: nevertheless I live; <u>yet not I, but Christ liveth in me</u>: and the life which I now live in the flesh I live by the faith of the Son of God, who loved me, and gave himself for me.**

Jesus continued, "I can spend all of your time here sharing this with you. I want your time here to change the way you see yourself with Me.

Heaven Awaits Your Expression

This star is fearfully & wonderfully made. Every detail has been intentionally placed within this star's makeup. You are seeing My workmanship. Look, you are created with many trillions of star-like atoms. You are created by my words. My words are spirit and they are life. My words are alive. I am the Word. I am the Life. I am the Light…the Light of the World. I uphold all things by the word of My power. I created you in My image. Your eyes look like My eyes. You are like Me. I AM like you.

Brock, you are aware that every single human on Earth has completely unique eyes? You know how entities scan the eyes, read fingerprints, and read DNA from people. Every person has their designed individuality and the expression of Me they were created to give. I know each by name. The stars as well. Now, watch the star _____ go back to doing the expression he was designed for."

He let it shoot right back up to its ordained place. Boom. Like that!

Hold it right there. Jesus let the star go…and said something. What did He say? I couldn't make out entirely what He said. Was I allowed to know? I didn't want to ask. I thought He would have called the star an "it". But he didn't. I think it was the Heavenly language of God. The star was called by name! Oh, the wisdom and knowledge of our God! He is omnipotent, omnipresent, and omniscient!

I cried again. Honestly, I can't even tell when I started or stopped crying. It is neither here nor there. It is the least of details. But I was emotional. I was crying. I loved crying before the Lord. It wasn't the same. Crying was amazing here! I felt like I just changed all over again. There went another expression of my King transmitted into my being. I was conformed into His image once again. I was becoming more like Him every single experience I had with Him.

It was becoming clear that THIS is what a relationship with Jesus was all about. This is what my relationship with Him should be like on Earth! I cried some more.

I was wide eyed and open mouthed. Eyes had tears beading up. The tears didn't affect my sight though. That was different. I knew I was crying, but nothing was too blurry. Hmmm. My mind just keeps being blown away!

I had scripture coming to me and I need to share some.

Daniel 12:3

³ And those who are wise shall shine like the brightness of the sky above; and those who turn many to righteousness, like the stars forever and ever.

The Spirit was showing me how even the righteous who reign with Jesus in eternity will be able to shine like the stars and the brightness of the sky above!

Proverbs 4:18 (KJV)

But the path of the just is as the shining light, that shineth more and more unto the perfect day.

Isaiah 60:1 (KJV)

Arise, shine; for thy light is come, and the glory of the Lord is risen upon thee.

Matthew 14:43 (KJV)

Then shall the righteous shine forth as the sun in the kingdom of their Father. Who hath ears to hear, let him hear.

CHAPTER 3

MY GUARDIAN ANGEL

*"The ferocious tenacity at which he moved with intent.
It put the fear of God in me overwhelmingly
like I've never felt before."*

Oh yeah, the angel! I turned to the left and there he was! It's true- I have an angel sent by God to serve me! Oh, amazement all over again.

I took in his tall posture. Ok, this is what I'm talking about! I guess I was believing Jesus' intentions toward me. He was consistently affirming his pleasure that I was there and demonstrated much loving acceptance towards me. He was pushing out permission for me to explore! I was in full trust! So, I decided to be a good son and act like myself. I could feel the joy from Jesus and the Spirit. Both were so one that I didn't know any difference at all. BUT, as soon as I had that thought, Jesus was speaking out loud this time.

"Brock, the same Spirit that raised Me from the dead, hovered on the face of the deep, and indwelled you since your new birth is in you now. Anytime you hear Me speaking inside of you, I'm speaking through the same Spirit. He is in you and in Me. Think of it as a window in your soul and a window in Mine. I speak to you from within Me and I can see and know all within you.

You as well; you have a window within you to speak to Me anytime. You have access to all of Me, all of My knowledge, power, presence, etc. You and I are one because of the Spirit within both of us.

I'm speaking to you outwardly now. Even this is by the Spirit of My Father. He speaks out of Me through the Spirit. We are all three one.

One window through each of us all acting outwardly as one in different roles. This is simple. You must not let this seem difficult. You are one with Me and we have NO DISTANCE between us. You are ever present with Me here in Heaven and I am ever present with you. I'm only as far as your call. I love you. I will never leave you nor forsake you. How could I forsake Myself?"

Scripture was pouring in!

1 Cor 6:17 (ESV)
> [17] But he who is joined to the Lord, becomes <u>one spirit with him.</u>

2 Timothy 2:12-13 (KJV)
> [12] But if we deny him, he will deny us; if we are faithless, he remains faithful- <u>for he cannot deny himself.</u>

John 17:20-23 (ESV)
> [20] "I do not ask for these only, but also for those who will believe in me through their word,
> [21] that they may all <u>be one, just as you, Father, are in me, and I in you</u>, that they also may be in us, so that the world may believe that you have sent me.
> [22] The glory that you have given me I have given to them, that they may be one even as we are one,
> [23] <u>I in them and you in me</u>, that they may become perfectly one, so that the world may know that you sent me and loved them even as you loved me…"

Heaven Awaits Your Expression

Oh, I was changed all over again. Expressions multiplied! Oh the bliss to be transformed by His words. His love, joy, & peace all in one flash. I continued crying. It made such perfect sense to me! I have just in one conversation had every question answered

I feel like I've ever had for the Lord. Oh, I'm just weak before Him. I wanted to just lay face down before Him.

But right then, I was turned by the Lord to see the angel.

I think the Lord knew that I'd be staying right there at His feet for all of eternity asking question after question after question! Oh, I wanted to feast at the feet of Jesus! I had so much I wanted to learn! I have already learned so much and had so much understanding from Him solidified that I felt like a whole new man!

So, I am turned, and I take in this tall angel. He was something else. He had a look like the blonde guy that played in the Hercules series when I was younger. He was bold cheeked and had what seemed to be a double chin. He had the look of one who has experienced more battles than any person in history. He seemed to be built to look ferocious. He was a weapon built for his job. He had a statue of a body. Oh man. I saw him like an image of what I'd like to be after much daydreaming of what possibilities were available to me if I worked out all day every day of my life! I thought, "Oh my…dude, you look so cool!" Ha-ha, here I was back to myself!

"You have golden hair!" I felt so comfortable with him. But I caught myself chuckling inside because I just spoke to a guy and praised the dude's hair. What in the World! Oh, I guess I was feeling so free here! His hair really was the coolest hair I've ever seen!

I was conversing with him like I have known him my whole life. I just walked up to Him, looked up high, and just started talking about how cool his hair was! His hair was made of gold. Not spray-painted gold. Not covered with gold. His hair was gold.

I said, "Your hair! It's so…gold! It's so cool- it flows down like it's almost alive."

Heaven Awaits Your Expression

He said the first thing to me, "Watch this. Watch what I can do with my hair."

I was taken back. He had such a strength to his voice. It was kind of scary. Not going to lie. Growing up by Ft. Campbell, working with Military, and in all my travels, I have talked to a lot of strong men, tough men, killers, the most elite warriors of the Earth, and powerful men.

This guy would make the Delta Force Units, the Navy Seals, CIA QRF, Spetsnaz, Polish Grom, Israeli Sayeret Matkal, and the toughest of SpecOps on the Earth think several times before they cross him. This isn't a guy I wouldn't even want to play wrestle with. I wouldn't want him to accidentally drop his long-armed hands on me. Ouch.

I was not only stunned by the strength of his voice, but the purity as well. It was like he has rarely talked in his life. He had such a purity to his voice. It was like conversation with me was the most amazing thing he's ever been told to do by the Lord in his whole created life. He had such purity, like that of a being who has served for millennia and has only rarely ever said anything outside of what his service required! It was so ordained talk that his words were just pure. It was talk that registered to me as pure, rare, and holy words.

Here I am talking to him like a brother in the Lord after an amazing worship encounter at church. I felt like we were fresh out of God's presence at church, both glowing with the aftereffects of the Lord's presence, and talking like brothers. Just talking and being bros.

This angel was excited to talk to me! That was fascinating to me! This angel is just as excited to talk to me as I am to him. How intriguing! I started to feel the "knowings" inside of me from the Lord again. I knew then that this angel has watched me my whole life. He's watched me, protected me, reported to me from the Lord, and observed me for the last 33 years. He's now getting to talk to me for the very first-time face to face!

I had some scripture flooding through me.

Psalm 91:11

> [11] **For he will command his angels concerning you <u>to guard you in all your ways.</u>**

Psalm 34: 7
> ⁷ The angel of the Lord <u>encamps around</u> those who fear him, and <u>delivers them</u>.

Psalm 130:20
> ²⁰ Bless the Lord, O you his angels, you <u>mighty ones</u> who <u>do his word, obeying the voice of his word</u>!

Exodus 23:20
> ²⁰ Behold, I send an angel before you <u>to guard you on the way</u> and <u>to bring you to the place that I have prepared</u>.

Daniel 6:22
> ²² My God sent his angel and <u>shut the lions' mouths</u>, and they have not harmed me…

Oh wow…this is just something beyond unbelievable! I am in Heaven, meeting Jesus for the first time fully, and seeing two angels that seem to be tasked to watch over me, bring knowledge, document what I do, bring any instructions Jesus needs for me to do. I'm just walking into Heaven and it's simply beyond my wildest dreams!

This angel responds to me to watch what he can do with his hair and I watch his long flowing golden hair move outward and quickly braid itself into some ancient warrior's braid. It reminded me of the old Samurai warriors who would braid their hair before battle.

When his hair came up and braided itself, I just looked up at him and said, "Wow, that is so awesome! Your hair goes up when you want it to? Whoa! Yeah, I can't do that on Earth!"

He chuckled, saying, "I've noticed. But you can do anything here. All things are Possible here."

I just stood there speechless.

As he stood there before me, I just stared speechless and then I saw the glimmer of an object behind his arm. I noticed his sword. He was turned sideways after showing me his hair and that's when I saw it!

He had a long sword…wait, no, he had two swords. I looked over and sure enough, he had two swords!

I said, "Whoa, your swords are the most stunning blades I've ever seen! But they're not at your waist! Every warrior I've seen on Earth has their swords at their hips or across their back! Your handles are underneath your arms! That's different!"

His swords had a slight curve backwards. They came down from close to his armpit downward to I'd say 6-8 inches past his fingertips.

This guy had long arms! He was 14-15 feet tall and had arms taller than my body! I'm 5' 8" & 3/4…and his sword was probably close to seven feet long! It was from his armpit down past his hands. Around his elbow, you could see the blade curving backwards. It finished its curve at the bottom under his hands. On the front side of his sword, it had curves with sharp tips, like a jagged edge going up the blade. It was a two-edged sword with both sides super sharp it seemed! I could tell it was a supernatural sword! It was a golden metal of some kind that we don't have on Earth. Golden Platinum. Put those two together and you may come closer. It's a lot like a sword you may find in a Marvel superhero movie. Some kind of weapon of the God kind!

Oh, I would love to learn about their weapons! I reminded myself to ask the Lord later!

I asked the angel, "Where is your sheath? How do you take them out? Where do you put them back in? Or how do they attach to you?

He said, "Look closely" and you will see. He held his arm forward as to show me the full sword underneath. There was a glimmer of a what looked like a sheath, but there wasn't one. I was like, "So there is a sheath? It's invisible?" He said, "No, my swords are not dangerous or sharp while they are by my side.

Once I pull them out to use them, they become extremely mighty in God to destroy. Anytime you need me, I use them like this…"

He stepped forward as if he was about to fight some invisible enemy. Oh wow. The ferocious tenacity at which he moved with intent. It put the fear of God in me overwhelmingly like I've never felt before.

I watched him reach with his right arm over to his left side, and simultaneously reach to his right side with his left arm. He crossed and the swords seemed to flow as one with him. They seemed to flex or move forward to make the grab flow seamlessly. He effortlessly became one with the blades! Thinking back, I thought he pulled the swords out of what we call on Earth a sheath. This was not like that.

These swords became one with his arms and he just crossed his arms and took sword and sword. He had them moving in impressive swipes of his wrists!

I shouted out loud without noticing it, "They are alive! Right? They have fire coming out of them or through them? You move so fast, I can't see."

He slowed a bit. I could hear a hum from the weapons. They seemed to buzz and had a light emulating from them. It reminded me of the stars I had saw in the eyes, and from God's Person on the Throne.

I said, "Wow, are they made of star? What do you do when someone shoots bullets at you?"

My brain was just puzzled. I immediately though of how silly that question was!

He grinned, and responded quickly, "Watch this," and he moved so fast and did a warrior's demonstration of spinning and swinging the swords with the grace of the most skilled dancers…a deadly fast warrior dancer. Oh, the speed! It reminded me of movies that showed elves in battle. They would move with such speed; you would see a trail of light behind them and they were the most graceful warriors in the different story's kingdoms.

This angel had the elves looking like kid's stories. It was beyond impressive! I knew, I never had to worry about any demon, person, or beast EVER. If this guy was with me, I was safe.

Hebrews 1:7

> **⁷ Of the angels he says, "He makes his angels <u>winds</u>, and his ministers <u>a flame of fire</u>."**

He finished. He slowed and walked toward me and said, "I don't typically fight enemies with bullets. Most of my fighting is with my hands up close. If an enemy shot at me, it would mean nothing. I can take out a whole army before they pull one trigger."

Then I remembered the story in the Bible:

2 Kings 19:35
> ³⁵ **And that night the angel of the Lord went out and <u>struck down 185,000</u> in the camp of the Assyrians. And when people arose early in the morning, behold, these were all dead bodies.**

Ok. Enough said. I had large eyes and I was jaw dropped. Nothing else was ever going to come out of me about this subject! I was trying to even process that information. Like seriously! What was I thinking?

This guy was not only extremely deadly, but I realized that he probably knows me more than anyone else on Earth. I was thinking about that. He has observed everything I've done. Whoa…that changes the way I'll make any decisions going forward! I knew God watched me…but this impressive being who could easily kill a whole army was with me, watching me!

I started thinking about the other angel. That other angel was literally documenting everything I did on a scroll or book. I could make out a book that he carried.

Daniel 4:13 (ESV)
> ¹³ "I saw in the visions of my head as I lay in bed, and behold, <u>a watcher, a holy one, came down from heaven</u>.
> ¹⁴ He proclaimed aloud and said…

Malachi 3:16 (ESV)
> ¹⁶ Then those who feared the Lord spoke with one another. The Lord paid attention and heard them, and <u>a book of remembrance was written before him</u> of those who feared the Lord and esteemed his name.

Heaven Awaits Your Expression

I don't think I was allowed to see that within the light I was seeing everything else. I'm sure God has a reason. I just know I won't ever see myself as being alone again.

The Holy Ghost, these angels, and I guess the cloud of witness are all looking at everything I do! Oh my. The responsibility! The scope of this position as a son of God. It's extremely important! It's not a little deal. It's huge. To be one of His sons. To know this, it brings such responsibility, such accountability, and I feel it's more of a team effort.

I now sense that so much of Heaven is in support to direct, lead, and provide for me in whatever God has me doing. The more you think of that, it begs the question: "What is too hard for the Lord? What is there that's impossible for God? What's impossible for me? Anything is possible. Anything!

The guardian angel warrior guy quickly crossed his arms and placed the deadly humming weapons back into their places.

He said, "These were created for me at the time of my birth. I was born of God with these same swords. They are one with me. I operate a lot like how I've seen you operate. I have abilities."

He kept speaking and pointed at me, "I've learned so much and thus increase the abilities God has designed me to do. Just as you grow in the grace abilities He's designed you to do. When you learn, practice, and do what you are designed to do, you increase in your abilities and responsibilities. That's how it is for me. I've served our Father for eternity. I've watched over many men. I'm tasked with my greatest honor now, to protect you. You are graced and chosen. I must watch over you and keep you in the Father's hands. Jesus will not lose even one of His lambs. He has assigned me to your everyday work. I am with you everywhere you go. As soon as you begin to pray, I stand in attention and the Spirit directs me to act. My Father's will is for me to act swiftly. I sometimes need help, especially when you pray in the Spirit. He always prays the will of the Father through you. Jesus and the Spirit have you pray as they pray. It's the most fascinating action you believers take.

Heaven Awaits Your Expression

It's so powerful. It moves so many of us in Heaven to work on Earth. Just one son of God moves so much activity in the Kingdom of Heaven. If all of the called-out ones would realize what we do when they pray, then wouldn't they pray more? For example, there's times when your prayers have me asking the Father for help. He always sends other angels to help.

The Holy Spirit has you crying out for revival. You are always praying for the Earth to be shaken with the Sons of God being fully awakened to their fullness in their Lord. You ask in your prayer language that you would walk in every known manifestation of the Spirit found within the Bible.

You ask to walk just as Jesus walked. You are constantly asking for those around you to be just as Jesus is. You are always asking for God to take you and show you the secrets of His kingdom. You are always asking Him to heal disabilities like no man has seen before. You are asking of great things that I've heard no man I've watched pray for. The Lord has you praying things that surely will cause the Hope of Your Salvation to come soon. This has me asking for help a lot. There are large fallen ones where you live. The demonic spirits amongst your neighbors. Demonic strongholds over your region have strong religious ties in the church."

He really had all of my attention!

He continued, "You should see the demonic activity amongst the churches! It is a horrible sight for me to see. I see what Jesus (he pronounced His name in a way that I can't even try to repeat) has done for the church with His own blood! I saw what He did to Satan! I saw the Body of Christ emerge from small beginnings. They are His Bride! They are heirs of God! They are His family! It hurts us to see them so crippled. They are not even alive...they are bodies and bodies of anemic souls. Their spirts are dead...having forms of godliness but they possess no power. They don't pray. We don't hear them. They have forms of self-appeasement in their times they call prayer. It's not the Family the Fathered willed into existence through Jesus when He formed Adam. It will not be like this for long."

The angel looked at me and then he looked at Jesus with a look of seeking permission from the Lord.

Heaven Awaits Your Expression

The Lord Himself was standing there this whole time listening with pure pleasure. I wondered what more could he say. This is already mind-boggling. My spirit was taking this all in...and holding back all of the questions forming.

I looked with the anticipation of what the angel was going to say. He again strengthened His posture. I was astonished by his light Bronze polished perfect skin.

He had such muscular features! His skin did something marvelous to behold. It sparkled, shimmered, with a gold shine...then to the resemblance of precious emerald stone. It was like his skin had elements of precious stones within it.

His beauty was unutterable. It had me standing and forgetting everything else. How does one's skin have so much expression? His skin was praising the Lord. His skin had its own way to worship the Lord! It was as if every part of him could express some of God's nature back to God in worship. Profound. Just marvelous! It invoked such genuine admiration of his individuality. He was an individual that The Father created and dearly loved like me. It bonded me with the angel. He was a part of my family. He was a part of my sacred tribe. He was with me and the Lord.

There was a special moment then. I had no idea, no scripture, no comprehension of any story like this. I started to rake through my studies over the years to draw up a reference to how me talking to the angel that was with me at all times made any sense.

I asked inside of me, "Lord, please help me here. I'm talking to the angel that you have assigned to me. How is this normal? How do I make sense of this?"

Gently, He said, "Son, you must understand, that you are talking to the angel who does My bidding for you, but it's not just him talking to you. The Spirit speaks through him as well. Each angel lives, moves, breathes, and has its being through the Spirit. He was merely moving and expressing what the Spirit wanted him to share. He simply did as his design is to do. He spoke to you what the Spirit desired you to hear.

Heaven Awaits Your Expression

You are with Me Brock. You will see more than this. With me, you must not wonder on such mysteries. In Heaven, you can talk to the gold, the water, the birds, the animals, the trees, and all angels. They can all communicate back. You can speak to all nationalities here. You can speak their language, and they can speak yours. There are no communication barriers here. There are many different types of angels. You will see much more than this. Just remember, you are experiencing this for the first time. Remember Zechariah in the Bible?

The whole book is about the prophet receiving instruction from an angel. He has full conversations with the angel. All through the Bible, I've given plenty of examples of my people having conversations with Angels. Remember Abraham?

Before I destroyed Sodom & Gomorra, I came with two angels. We had a conversation. This is as I have it. Let's continue..."

He looked at the angel as if it's his turn now.

The angel looked at me with knowing, ancient, wise eyes. He said, "Brock, you will learn more of me in the future. Your future is before me. I see what you are to accomplish by the Lord's direction. I will see you when you visit Heaven.

I'll be eager to show you around. You must humble yourself and seek the Lord at all times. I can't help you like I want to without you yielding to Him wholeheartedly in prayer. You can do way more on the Earth if you pray with passionate intention. When you pray, I get the one thing I'm most passionate about- bringing Heaven's realties to Earth's people. It is my greatest privilege! Also, I enjoy battling. Don't ever think it is scary, or a nuisance to us.

WE LOVE TO WAR AND FIGHT THOSE WHO REBELLED AGAINST OUR WAY.

It brings Joy to our order to bring justice any moment we can in the name of the Holy One.

Heaven Awaits Your Expression

Jesus has defeated all. He has all authority. You can pray anything in His name, and it is done by your Father. It may take time, but every prayer is heard and acted upon! Listen, you have an opportunity to see the Father! I'm honored to take you into His presence. He wants you to see His eye. I will take you to the place he has set for you"

Heaven Awaits Your Expression

CHAPTER 4

THE FATHER'S GLORY

"It was like the sun was pressed up against my being and I was forced to survive the terror.."

It all happened so fast. I was whipped up and wow was he strong! Boom…we were there. I couldn't hear myself think…it was so loud! It was Earth quaking thundering loud. The angel had his hand on my shoulder, and I knew there was no way for me to even survive being in this spot if it wasn't for him! I couldn't see God anywhere. Just light and streaks of light. I realized later that I was standing by lightning strikes! It was electricity in the purest form. I don't know much about electricity other than the basics, but this seemed to be electricity shooting out everywhere. Creative lightning charging out everywhere. I didn't feel like I was by the person of the Father. I feel like in my abilities to know things in Heaven, I sensed I was STILL miles from His throne. I feel like I was going to die here, and I was still miles away…oh my soul. Bless the Lord oh my soul! Oh, how Great is His Love!

I started to sing a spontaneous song! I sang Holy is the Lord! Holy is the Lord God Almighty! I sang from my heart songs I've never heard.

Heaven Awaits Your Expression

I wanted to burst with my body exploding everywhere. I literally felt if my body exploded it would be my best worship to the Lord. How do I explain that? Beyond me...I was caught up in an ecstasy that had my mind in a completely new place! I wanted to be right here forever! I was conscious of the moments of peace between each heartbeat. How? I don't know...but I was super aware of every particle within my body and soul. I was aware of every vibration. I was aware of the Father's energy talking into my being. It was as if He was singing and speaking to me, over me, because of me, about me, and for me? I was instantly picturing myself holding my son and my daughter as infants and toddlers. We would sing a song to them as they would fall asleep. The love I felt for my kids as I held them and took in their features. That's a glimpse of how I felt the Lord was feeling over me right now!

He was...he had no cause to have explanation. He is so supreme. He is so powerful that I wanted to just be flat on the floor. The floor was so crystal clear that I couldn't tell if I was on sky or on a floor. It wasn't glass either. It was crystal-like; It had what seemed to be layers of crystal, some diamond, some transparent like gold, and some other gem like material that was translucent/transparent. It was vibrating...I could not hear a hum, but I knew it had one. It was like giving off a specific frequency...some level of sound that was unheard of.

I tried to breathe in air while thinking this quickly. I couldn't breathe. Well, maybe it was a frequency that God was pleased with and the floor was praising Him as well? All I knew was- I can't breathe out of my mouth. I realized that there was not a struggle like on the Earth. On Earth, my face would turn red and I'd panic! Here, it's life. I was taking on meaning from this experience...Hmmm. There's no death in Heaven! It's not possible to die in Heaven! I was unable to breathe out of my mouth and lungs but in His presence, I didn't need to operate the same way! In Him I breathe...oh my wonders...I didn't have to breathe! Wow...that's probably why my heartbeat was so noticeable- perhaps I didn't even need the beat of my heart within his presence! WOW...my God! My Father!

Heaven Awaits Your Expression

It's all about Him! Everything is to glorify Him! Everything Jesus did and does is to glorify Him! The Holy Spirit glorifies Him!

Acts 17:28

²⁸ For <u>in Him we live, and move, and have our being</u>; as certain also of your own poets have said, For we are also his offspring.

Oh, I was unaware of the surroundings. I think I was only there for a couple of seconds and all this was permeating my being. Maybe I was there for hours?? I have no idea.

Suddenly, I'm held up quickly and held forcefully to stand as an unbearable explosion, implosion, fusion, something supernova was brightly bursting before me. I saw all around me the unlimited brightness of colors, light, and star fire. It was like the sun was pressed up against my being and I was forced to survive the terror. The atmosphere trembled, the air itself was having an earthquake. The lightning wasn't the earthly lightning. This lightning was flowing out from a mighty spiral of some sort from the sun. I couldn't even try to describe His eye to you. I will mess it up. I just know that it was the most powerful of sun stars. His eyes were everything of everything. It was unendurable for me. I wanted away and yet stay there forever. I was yielding my spirit to be with Him forever. I thought I couldn't take any more.

I must give Him my everything. I thought this was the only way to die. I didn't exactly feel as though I would die. But there's no words to describe the powerful urge to surrender all of my knowing to Him. Everything that was a thought, from the beginning of my life until now, was laid bare before Him. I was never so naked in my life. My thoughts felt as though they had no clothes. There was nothing to hide before the Creator. There was love. There was power. There was grace and mercy. There was justice. Judgement and Mercy were eternally bursting out of His being. I can't believe I was here. Was I still here?

Heck, I don't remember time anymore because I felt as though all of me was given.

Heaven Awaits Your Expression

All of me passed on to Him and nothing was left for me to claim. Oh, the experience was overwhelming. I obviously didn't die!

I was still alive! The angel yanked me abruptly out of the exchange and instantly I found myself collapsed before Jesus. Oh, I was relieved and in a state of holy shock. Being in awestruck wonder of the might of our God. There are no words. I knew I was different. Here I was, in expression overload. Transforming, birthing, and resurrection life - these are the words that came out of my word bank. I had a knowing.

==I would be **ONLY HIS** for eternity.==

I was undone before Jesus. Low. I had emotion unknown to me freely living within my being. I'm not sure it was even an emotion. Who knows truly what was moving and sizzling within my newly renewed soul? It was more like a spreading awareness of God in me. Not so much the awareness that He exists...this was more alive than that. I was enlightened with the realization that I was of God and from God. I was not separate from God. I was completely formed from every atom of my being in the complete and full likeness of the Almighty God. I was here soaking in this experience. I just wanted Jesus. Nothing or No-one else. Jesus and Jesus alone. I was absorbed into the reality that I was made, created, shaped, formed, painted, and destined to be in union for all of eternity with Jesus! I was home. Oh, if I could just stay here forever! Forget going back!

Finally, I could just be at Jesus's feet! Oh, that's all I wanted! All of this was shattering everything I have ever known. There's not one Sunday school lesson, sermon preached, book read, worship service, or prayer meeting to ever prepare me for this. I felt He shook everything in me out of me. I felt like I was just done...spent. I just laid there before Jesus. Not a word. Not a cry. Not a whisper.

Just the complete awareness of my heart still beating. It was still beating. Or was it? Did hearts even beat in Heaven? Did they even have to? I just knew that I still had my Earthly mind operating some. It's a mystery to me.

I was still alive. I was in shock, terror, and in holy awe. I was amazed. Really, God the Father scared and excited me all the same. I was never to see God the same!

~

May all those who have ears to hear be hungry enough to pursue truly knowing God intimately, up close and personal! Oh, may you burn with a holy fire that has taken all of my living to a dead surrender. May you experience what it is to be a "living sacrifice" as Paul referred to in Romans 12. As the fire of God came down from Heaven's realm and consumed the oxen sacrificed on the altar of Elijah before all the prophets of Baal…may your soul be fully consumed before the mighty consuming presence of God Almighty! Consume the Word of God until the Word of God consumes you!

1 Kings 18:38-39 (KJV)
> Then the **<u>fire of the Lord fell, and consumed</u>** the burnt sacrifice, and the wood, and the stones, and the dust, and **<u>licked up the water that was in the trench</u>**. And when all the people saw it, they **<u>fell on their faces</u>**: and they said, The Lord, he is the God; the Lord, he is the God.

I pray you will encounter Him right now! Today! Not someday…but right now! I pray His presence overwhelms you right now! His Spirit yearns jealously over you and wants to accomplish His mission with you - to Glorify the Son and the Father. He wants to manifest Himself to you and to others through you! Let him! Oh, yield and allow Him to lead and guide you into this most holy walk with Him!

Please. Take this time to lift your hands, thank Him, sing to Him, bow to Him, praise Him, and seek His face! Don't let this moment pass and not let the Spirit of God manifest the presence of God to you right now!

Heaven Awaits Your Expression

If you don't know Him personally, then stop what you are doing and call upon the name of Jesus and repent with all your heart! Stop living your life for yourself.

Die to all of your ways, all of your selfish desires, and decide once and for all that Jesus will be King of every area of your life. He must be King, the one Lord, and the Supreme RULER of your life!

There can be no other in your life BUT HIM. He cannot be #2. He cannot be behind anything or anyone in your life. Including you. You must deny yourself and choose Him to be before you in ALL of your ways.

He must be your ALL. If you doubt that your life is completely surrendered to Him…if there's any doubt at all- make it right. Right now. Make it right.

He is God. He will judge you one day. You will stand before Jesus, the books will be opened, and the works of your life will be out in the open.

If you have not made Him #1 and made Jesus Lord of your life and changed your life to be obedient to Him…then you will have a scary eternity screaming constantly while your flesh burns off your bones over and over and the one thing you will remember for all eternity, is reading this Book and knowing you were given a chance.

Make that right. Do it now. Oh, don't read this book and see what awaits believers in eternity and in the end fail to walk through the veil and be in eternity with Jesus!

Oh, I beg you to let Jesus make Himself known to you!

After you pray, go to the next chapter, and let's continue on…

CHAPTER 5

THE TREES, FLOWERS, AND WATER

"The tree was spread out and was at the same time bowing to the Lord, giving out its expression in worship to Jesus, and honoring Him.."

So, there I was, before the feet of Jesus! I'm not even sure how long I've been seeing into Heaven at this point. I could still feel an awareness that I was sitting on my couch and staring at the Christmas tree…and yet I was here before Jesus. My spirit was on fire! My heart was beating and adrenaline rushing on my couch. I was aware of these things and yet seeing with the eyes of my spirit this whole ordeal.

I begin to think again. I thought to myself quickly, "I see now why there's such a thing as the Trinity. God the Father, who creates an innumerable number of universes and worlds holds the universes in His hands. He is power untold. He is not magic. He is. He simply IS. There's not a thing we can imagine that wasn't made by Him. The Father is great and mighty and terrible and wondrous. He is so powerful! But thank goodness the Son Jesus was so pleasant to be close to! Hmm, how is that? Why? Is Jesus a different expression of the Trinity? He is the express image of God and the fulness of the Godhead bodily. Perhaps different jobs.

Like the sun. The Father is like the burning hot, deathly, and ferocious ball of fire as we know the Sun in our galaxy is. The Son Jesus is the light of the world coming from that ball of burning sun. The Spirit is the warmth, heat, & Sunburn you feel and experience?"

Then I realized, "Well, actually, Jesus can shine bright as the sun too! The apostle John saw Him and fell as a dead man too! He shined so bright his hair was white as snow! I remembered Jesus on the Mount of Transfiguration (Matt 17) as well. He was bright as the sun then! Every angel did too!"

Oh, what do I know? Forget everything I just thought! Oh my…it must be Mercy! Oh, that is it! He's just allowing me to approach Him. Oh, it's just the mercy of God that I'm able to lay here at the feet of Jesus! Ugh, I am going to stop thinking!

How can you describe the greatness of God? His mercy is everlasting! I understood Mercy like it was the first time I've learned. It was a new concept to me. Mercy to me on Earth, growing up in America was just a small meaning to me. I needed to repent all over again. I felt a sense of being dirty or unclean and needful of His mercy all over again.

But then again, I was able to think of me on Earth as different from what I was experiencing in the moment. I could sense a whole larger concept of Mercy than what I had conceived on Earth. Oh, His Mercy is much more! We have the privilege of being up close and personal with Him! That is called mercy. He has compassion on us and allows us to approach Him as bold as a kid is free to run and jump in the arms of their parents! We can run into Abba's arms and be within the heartbeat of His bosom…and not be deathly evaporated into oblivion. We are favored! We are truly one with Him. We are family. We are Sons and Daughters. We are His Bride! There are no other words in the Earthly experience to show love and intimacy!

Marriage intimacy is sexual closeness and the most holy intimacy known to mankind. The love of family is the next closest!

Heaven Awaits Your Expression

Friendship, family, spouse, etc. are all the sweetest areas of closeness a person can look forward to within their lifetime!

But…to experience all of that in personal encounters, in relationship, in oneness, and in a pure union with God almighty is beyond our minds.

I cried. Oh, I was losing my concept of time and the audience watching me. Oh, I had no qualms about crying and sobbing in front of a thousand strangers right here. I could sense that my tears were pouring from my eyes!

Time was non-existent. I just cried as Mary did in the Bible. I didn't have an alabaster box, but I had tears! I didn't have long hair to wipe the tears…but I just cried.

Jesus lifted me up. The tears were gone. He touched me. Beautifully. Sweetly, like honey flowing over my face I received strength, courage, and a sound mind. I was alert. Focused, attentive, and surprisingly able to stand on my feet!

Jesus looked at me. I pulled in from His being all the love, joy, and peace I could contain. He knew I needed it. I was taking in His energy. I was taking in His strength. There I was, standing with Jesus Christ. The shock was more behind me now. I was of the mindset that I wanted to be here forever. I wanted to leave my body behind and stay here!

Jesus smiled a knowing care filled look and said,
"Brock, I am with you. I'm right here.
I have more to show you. Come."

~

We started to walk. I was near the center of the golden walkway. The aurora of God the Father's presence was lighting up the whole world of Heaven coming from my far distant left. The radiant color display of nebula star dust glory clouds filled the sky like a beautiful sunset with a whole color show to go with it.

It was like the mix of a supernova star display, the most beautiful sunset I've ever seen, and the expanse of stars in and beyond all of that! Oh, it was wonderful...all laid out like an artist's greatest work- just laid out before me to gaze at!

The guardian angel with the amazing warrior swords and dazzling skin and golden hair was walking courteously to my left, just slightly behind me. He's like a ninja. Seriously! How can you be that big and walk so softly quiet right beside me? Made me fill with lots of curious questions to ask the Lord later. I wonder if I could practice that on Earth?

Jesus was walking in front of me and to the right on the golden pathway. The tall slender angel was somewhere, I think. I didn't really take the time to see him again after noticing Jesus. I just knew that he was present and seemed to be on my back right.

I wanted to watch Jesus walk. I wanted to see His posture as He walked. Did He carry himself in a way I've watched great leaders walk on the Earth? I've seen many so-called great men of God in my day. I've eagerly and watchfully watched them walk, interact with others, pray for people, listen to people, laugh with others, correct folks, eat, drink, and socialize. I've been a student of men of God whom I felt I was supposed to learn from. Even guys who weren't exactly preachers, but honest Christian businessmen as well. I've studied their people skills with a passion! I've always wanted to be great with people! I've sat in airports for hours and just watched people! I love watching and observing folks! Today, right now, I can't believe my eyes!

I am observing the Living Water walk. The Bread of Life. He's the King of Kings and Lord of Lords.

I cannot fully describe how I was perceiving His walking because I kept getting distracted! I've never seen anything nearly close to what I was seeing! I watched as every step Jesus took made the ground vibrate around Him.

The grass was waving, praising, and giving forth their most beautiful expression to the Lord!

I was just dumbfounded...the grass was alive and praising the Lord! I watched...speechless.

Heaven Awaits Your Expression

Jesus stopped walking.

"What do you see?" Jesus asked me. He knew I was looking at the grass still as I stopped with Him. He turned to the direction of my observing with me.

I looked past Jesus. There was dimness around my peripheral and light centered in my sights. I could see trees, flowers, the stream of water flowing. I didn't answer because I was trying to see more out of what was dimmed in my vision. Light was clearing more and more of my sight as I willed myself to see. It was like I had to try to see. My mind just seemed to take in details, and it took time for things to process through my Earthly experiences and knowledge. I just don't know how to properly describe the effort my brain was awakening to. It's just different. The Light was different. The light was just everywhere. Light was lighting up everything. I just processed and kept surveying the landscape. I couldn't put my finger on it. What was I trying to identify?

Jesus asked again, "What do you see?"

"Lord, ok, yeah, sorry Lord. I see the trees over there, I see the flowers right there, the grass all over, the water flowing through, and there's light. Lord, the light! Oh, it's not like anything I've experienced ever! I still see the light reflecting from the Father's light and the star's reflections upon the living water. It's so bright! I've never seen anything like this! There's absolutely light everywhere. On all sides of the trees I see light. Whoa! Hold up!"

I paused and processed. I was starting to get the hang of this. He was in my thoughts. I paused in my thoughts, looked shortly at Him. He willed back at me saying, "Yes... keep going."

With that, I knew I was on the proper train of thought! I was having to second guess my eyes! I was not seeing any shadows! There was no shade under the trees! No shade! No shadows. No darkness. Light was fully wrapped around everything! How do you explain that?

Heaven Awaits Your Expression

I gawked with my whole being seeming to be eyeing everything at the same time. I said, "Lord, there's no shade at all. No darkness. Nothing but light here!"

Jesus, smiling and nodding. He was enjoying this!

I was interrupted with an overwhelming emotion inside bubbling up inside of me. I just couldn't look at Jesus more than a moment and just keep myself together! I was feeling the same gush of glory from deep within me calling out to the deep…the depths of the Maker I was beholding. His eyes were reflecting more than they were last time! It was a newness flowing out of me. He seemed to birth revelation in me and simultaneously the insides of me seemed to transform. I felt like a was an animal molting. Like I was shedding off old skin. Losing old feathers? I was being renewed every time I looked at Jesus.

Jesus smiled, and began to hold His hands outwardly as to show me that He was now taking the moment and teaching me. He was about to speak. He was now fathering me.

I was His Son, sitting with bugged out eyes adoring my hero father and ready to explode with excitement before the most amazing adventurous story I could ever imagine hearing! The emotion inside of me knew I was becoming one all over again! I was too enamored with His eyes to think further…i just waited. I stood there with my hands doing their own thing. I think my hands were up in worship. I wasn't sure. I could see Him with my inward knowing ability, but my outward eyes had tears in them blurring the reality of everything in my vision.

I was just shedding off everything I understood about Jesus and His Heavenly realities. Oh, I can't go two moments with Jesus without being transformed! I have to stop and allow the welling up of this glory within me come up out of my being, it comes out in tears, in worship, in adoration…hands held high in surrender to the next words coming out of His mouth.

Jesus began to open His mouth,

Heaven Awaits Your Expression

"Listen Brock, I'm sharing eternal truths. Listen closely. You have eyes, ears, and other senses you use on Earth to interpret the realities of what surrounds you there. Your eyes translate the reflections of colors into meanings within your mind. Your ears process the vibrations and placement you find yourself within at any moment. Your nose catches and filters the surrounding particles passing into your body from the air. Your mouth tastes, chews, and breaks down what you are allowing to enter your stomach. Your skin absorbs what's interacting with your body, protects your insides, and gives many signals if your environment makes contact with your body. These are your senses. You have other senses on Earth. You have many more we can discuss. Your body was created to read the interaction you have with all life forms on Earth. Your Earthly body was originally created with every capability to connect with the grass, the trees, the water, and communicate with them all. What you see here Brock, is how I created the Earth originally.

How you see, know, smell, hear, talk, feel, understand, move, etc. is all how I created the Earthly bodies of humans to function. I created Adam as my body. Think of what Paul taught about the glorified body you will receive when I return. Remember? Immortality swallows up your mortal body. You will take off your Earth suit tainted with death and sin and put on a body where you will see Me face to face and be known as you truly are. Go back and study those. I'm allowing you to see what the Heavenly experience is like. You are to learn of these realities, learn of my original intent, and allow Me to share these truths with you."

I had scripture coming to me.

1 Cor 15:51-53 (KJV)

⁵¹ Behold, I shew you a mystery; We shall not all sleep, but we shall all be changed,

⁵² In a moment, in the twinkling of an eye, at the last trump: for the trumpet shall sound, and the dead shall be raised incorruptible, and we shall be changed.

⁵³ For this corruptible must put on incorruption, and this mortal must put on immortality.

Heaven Awaits Your Expression

He paused. I spoke up, "Lord, please teach me. Please!"
He pointed, "You see that tree?"
I nodded as I looked expectantly.
He said, "Watch the tree" and that's exactly what I did. How could I not?
The tree turned all his branches toward Jesus, slightly to the tree's right. As if I was watching some fantasy movie, the tree turned toward Jesus spreading out the branches in a unique spread towards the Lord. The tree's leaves all turned outward and wide as if to take in all the light from the Son of God before it and seemed to breathe in the Lord. The tree was spread out and was at the same time bowing to the Lord, **giving out it's expression in worship to Jesus, and honoring Him**. Wow!

The tree was alive! The tree did what I would see trees on Earth do very slowly. Trees and plants move toward the light of the sun. They move and grow towards the light! This tree was FULLY ALIVE! This tree did in a moment what trees on Earth take hours or days to do! I realized that when we shoot video on Earth in "time lapse" format, we are showing in full speed what trees do close to their normal speed in Heaven! Oh, my goodness - the revelation was hard to handle! I was visualizing the many documentaries and YouTube videos I've watched with plants sprouting out of the ground, trees growing, vines opening up into curly hands and grabbing for a further reach! I could see Earthly memories play before my eyes. I realized what the Fall has done on the Earth. It has caused plants to truly be stuck in the futility of their suffering after Adam sinned and brought death into the Earth! Before Adam sinned, he was living HEAVEN ON EARTH! Jesus was showing me His Heavenly design! Oh, the weight of the moment was thick. I was all ears!

Jesus did something quite amazing! I watched Him now. The tree was just amazing, but, then I had an intuition that I must watch the other side of this exchange. Jesus was standing there and taking in the worship from the tree! Whoa…wait! Jesus was receiving the worship from the tree? Jesus had recently just received my worship! He was now receiving worship from a…. yeah…a tree!

The tree. I looked at the tree.
It was shaking the edges of its smaller branches and rattling in praise, **giving all the being could give.**

I had so many scriptures from the Lord coming through my mind.
1 Chronicles 16:31-33 (KJV)
³¹ Let the heavens be glad, and let the earth rejoice: and let men say among the nations, The Lord reigneth.
³² Let the <u>sea roar</u>, and the fulness thereof: let the <u>fields rejoice</u>, and <u>all that is therein</u>.
³³ Then shall <u>the trees of the woods sing out at the presence of the Lord</u>, because he cometh to judge the earth.

Isaiah 55:12 (ESV)
¹² "For you shall go out in joy and be led forth in peace; the mountains and the hills before you shall break forth into singing, and <u>all the trees of the field shall clap their hands</u>.

Jesus. He was just standing there with hands open taking in with pleasure the expression this tree was created to give to Him. Taking it in. Then suddenly, Jesus, with the movement of a symphony composer directing the most intimate of displays in a tapestry of art before my eyes - He opened his arms. He did what I interpreted as His turn now to give back to the tree! He opened His arms, and WOOSH...THE TREE BLEW UPWARD with all branches, leaves, erect and outward in the fullest expression the tree could put out. The tree shined with a greener gloss, orange colors radiating every vein of the leaves! How could I see the veins? Lord only knows! The leaves were receiving color, art, and glory within every vein it seemed! The bark was glossing over! Buds were shooting and flowers were rapidly blossoming, and the insides of the flowers were shooting forth and releasing a sweet fragrance to all the plants nearby! It was this tree's fullest expression to give to the Lord.

Heaven Awaits Your Expression

The flowers on the ground caught this...like electricity, all the plants around the tree were instantly shocked! It was contagious!

The next tree erupted in a self-explosive display of praise, pollination, and blossoming!

The flowers below all the trees and coming out of the tree line towards the grass and water stream all instantly, as if in a wave, were shocked into the contagious praise!

It was an invisible ripple of light, fragrance, sound, and energy on all sides of that one tree! The flowers all blossomed in succession and gave off the most beautiful display of color and garden beauty I've ever seen!

I've watched videos capturing the time lapse of gardens full of flowers blossom and this was so instant and all full of God's Spirit! It wasn't just the springtime blossom season! It was a worship service conducted out from within these alive beings...out of the flowers, who all are full of the Spirit of God like I am! I watched as all the flowers blossomed radiant unfolding pedals and bent as one body towards the outstretched Son of Almighty God!

I watched the next tree do the most amazing dance! It was a tree doing a dance! How in the world do I put this on paper!?? The tree was a mix of a metallic grey bark and a marble stone on the trunk and branches. The branches outreached like massive arms outward kind of like wild stretched out fig trees but with the age of the planet Earth probably! It was ancient, I could tell! The tree had the unique look of a fig tree mixed with some of the beauty of Japanese Maples and had the beautiful branches/leaves as a Weeping Willow tree! I was thinking all of this so rapidly, taking in this information, with a download of details instantly, as I watched the tree wave its branches toward Jesus, and made waves with its weeping leaves/branches!

The tree reminded me of Pocahontas. The large Weeping Willow tree that she would talk to. Try to imagine that tree, but with each downward flowing branch was a blue green starting off (the leaves were that color) but once it worshipped, all the leaves turned into flowers! Pink flowers! Milky pink. Like the pink of Himalayan salt and ivory...just a big tree with outstretched arms worshipping Jesus!

Heaven Awaits Your Expression

The tree looked like it had long flowing pink hair!

The tree gave off a most unique dance, wave of its hair, and a very sweet sound. The branches rattled in a chorus.

The tree had its own rhythm, beat, a song from all its parts moving in symphony. The tree was an individual!

The tree was loved by God! The tree loved God back- just like I do. Oh, I just marveled at this display of Heavenly bliss! Then I noticed how the trees and the flowers, and the waves in the grass, and the fountain shooting water all worked in a praise assembly towards the Holy One of Israel. The Lamb of God. He truly is God Almighty! How am I even allowed to be here and see this!!?

The water danced in shots of fountain like dances! Active, energized, and gushing up in a life like praise of its own!

Psalm 96:11-13 (ESV)

> [11] Let <u>the heavens</u> be glad, and let <u>the earth rejoice</u>; let <u>the sea roar, and all that fills it;</u>
>
> [12] let the <u>field</u> exult, and <u>everything in it</u>! Then shall all the <u>trees of the forest sing</u> for joy
>
> [13] before the Lord, <u>for he comes</u>…

Psalm 148:1-13 (KJV)

> [1] Praise ye the Lord. Praise ye the Lord <u>from the heavens: praise him in the heights.</u>
>
> [2] Praise ye him, <u>all his angels: praise ye him, all his hosts.</u>
>
> [3] Praise ye him, sun and moon: praise him, <u>all ye stars of light</u>.
>
> [4] Praise him, ye <u>heavens of heavens</u>, and ye <u>waters that be above the heavens.</u>
>
> [5] Let them praise the name of the Lord: for he commanded, and they were created.
>
> [6] He hath also stablished them for ever and ever: he hath made a decree which shall not pass.
>
> [7] Praise the Lord from the earth, ye dragons, and all deeps:

> **⁸ Fire, and hail; snow, and vapours; stormy wind fulfilling his word:**
> **⁹ Mountains, and all hills; <u>fruitful trees, and all cedars:</u>**
> **¹⁰ <u>Beasts, and all cattle; creeping things, and flying fowl:</u>**
> **¹¹ Kings of the earth, and all people; princes, and all judges of the earth:**
> **¹² Both young men, and maidens; old men, and children:**
> **¹³ Let them praise the name of the Lord: for his name alone is excellent; <u>his glory is above the earth and heaven.</u>**

~

I felt like I was tripping. This was too amazing. I'm watching this and my natural mind has just died and came back to life! I can see this with the Heavenly abilities I am experiencing within the vision, but my natural mind who is taking this in as well on my couch was having trouble letting this vision settle with it.

~

The Lord knew what was happening and He willed for the display to slow down. So, the animals did a beautiful slowing down of the jubilee before me.

This had me in awe. I've been in countless worship moments on the Earth where you truly are in God's presence. Each time you are singing in an assembly of believers, you have your hands lifted, eyes closed, singing, and at some point, you are just full to overflowing with God's presence. It's that warm, peace, love, joy, embrace, freedom, etc. that accompany each experience in the Lord's presence. I know each time, when I'm crying in worship, and I have already brought my need, concern, or pain to the Lord, He always touches me in that moment and the weight is lifted.

My mind feels lighter and the free weightless joy and position of my mind and soul in worship brings me into a closeness with the Lord that truly is the most precious place I can express with words I enjoy.

Heaven Awaits Your Expression

It's close to what one experiences in sex, in a high from drugs, the thrill on a roller coaster, or the drunken looseness of alcohol's buzz. It's way more than that, but accompanied with a peace unexplainable, a joy unspeakable, and love uncontainable. It's accompanied by the Spirit of God touching all of your Earthly senses and the voice of the Spirit speaking to you. All of which happens between you and the Lord. It's a relationship. It's a moment you get to experience with each other. That moment is private.

I had all this surfacing before me. The Lord was affirming me inside, acknowledging the information retrieval I was pulling on inside of my mind. He just watched as I realized the depth of what He was showing me.

Ephesians 5:18 (KJV)
> **18 And be not drunk with wine, wherein is excess; <u>but be filled with the Spirit</u>;**

I went back to my memories of those worship experiences. I remembered how after a number of glorious encounters with the Lord in worship, the latter portion of the experience would leave the whole congregation in a quiet still peaceful moment, where all would come to a shhhh, and everyone would just bask in the atmosphere of Heaven present. Everyone would just be still and know that He is God. Everyone would not move a muscle. That's what's happening right before me.

The plants, trees, the water, the grass, the air around where we were standing, and even myself was now caught up in this moment. We ALL as one began to be pulled into a holy hush before our Creator. We had thoughts of gratitude and thanks rushing through us. We were all feeling the same impulses. I could somehow understand this. We were all in such unity with the Spirit that we worshiped the Father and Son as one body.

Oh, it was sweet. It had a sound of purity…no sound at all. But the silence was itself a sound of beauty to the Lord.

There was a smell of a perfect mix of all fragrancies being moved by the wind toward everyone. Not just the Lord- but everyone was taking in the smells of the moment. It was its own unique moment. No other moment in eternity would give this experience.

It was a moment of time that each and every individual being experienced together. Each being experienced personal dignity coming from the Lord and the other creatures. Not like we typically treat beings on Earth. Earth people don't typically treat the grass, trees, flowers, water, air, soil, etc. with this kind of individual dignity. It was beyond my capacity to hold within me.

Psalm 150:6 (ESV)
¹⁸ Let <u>everything that has breath</u> praise the Lord! Praise the Lord!
Revelation 5:13 (ESV)
¹³ And I heard <u>every creature</u> in heaven and on earth and under the earth and in the sea, and all that is in them, saying, "To him who sits on the throne and to the Lamb be blessing and honor and glory and might forever and ever!"

I cried all of my tears out again. I was transformed again! Renewed again. I shed off all the discovered knowledge I thought I knew about the Lord and His creation. I realized that every single thing the Lord taught me had me transformed from glory to glory. I would see Him in a fresh way each and every time. New. Fresh. New Expressions. I'm wholly and completely blown away all over again. I felt more LIKE Him every time I experienced Him.

Colossians 3:10
¹⁰ And have put on the new man, which is <u>renewed in knowledge after the image of him that created him</u>:

Each time I felt more able to understand Him and think together with Him as we walked, looked, and spoke together. We were becoming more and more in sync with each experience. I was starting to understand more! I was feeling a whole mass of new revelation flood out from within me.

Heaven Awaits Your Expression

I was having more Ah hah moments and more epiphany moments! More light was connecting eternal dots within my mind!

I was being here with the Lord and looking at Him and what He instructed me to behold. What He showed me. What He guided me into, taught me, and unveiled to me was causing me to see so much of His design, His identity, His ways, His heart, and His love. I was truly being changed into the same image from each glory to the next glory! (2 Cor 3:18) I wasn't changed from seeing only His glory, but I was changed by seeing the Glory of Him who was being expressed out of each and every one of His creation around me.

Oh, His holiness was beautiful! I was present to see all the Heavens declare the Glory of God! They all soaked up His peace! They all were transformed as they experienced His presence too! It made me wonder if on Earth the trees would still respond to His presence as well? Perhaps slower, but I wondered how that would look.

Jesus knew my thoughts. He asked me, "Do you remember those videos you watched of the water showing different shapes and patterns with different music played around it? Remember the way music would react to different words spoken to it? Do you remember the science study they did on rice that had positive words spoken to it and the rice that had negative words spoken to it?"

Well of course I remembered! As soon as he spoke of the memories, He had them right up in the forefront of my mind. There was a video that proved how water had memory. Each played in quick succession showing me that even the beings on Earth respond to our words, our praise, and our presence! WOW!

"Lord, I want to learn more! I want to treat the trees, the plants, the grass, the water, the birds, the livestock, my chickens, my dog, etc. the way you treat them here! Oh Lord! This is beautiful! It's perfect! It's the way we were designed!

Colossians 1:15-19 (KJV)
15 Who is the <u>image of the invisible God</u>, the firstborn of every creature:

¹⁶ For by him were <u>all things created,</u> that are in heaven, and that are in earth, visible and invisible, whether they be thrones, or dominions, or principalities, or powers: all things were created by him, and for him:

¹⁷ And he is <u>before all things, and by him all things consist.</u>

¹⁸ And he is the head of the body, the church: who is the beginning, the firstborn from the dead; <u>that in all things he might have the preeminence.</u>

¹⁹ For it pleased the Father that <u>in him should all fulness dwell.</u>

CHAPTER 6

THE HEAVENLY JERUSALEM

"I could see those rivers that flowed forth from the Mountain in each direction and flowed outwardly to all of the Planet Heaven!"

Jesus motioned for me to come closer,
"Brock, let me show you My Eden.
You should see how nature thrives here!
You will love to see this in its fullness!"

    I did not even say a word. I was so excited! I have been watching videos on "Back to Eden" and have afterwards called tree companies to bring me woodchips. For three years, I have had tree companies bring me wood chips for my gardens. I've desired to grow food forests on my properties and design a sustainable property that mimicked nature's sustainable methods. Hence, that is why I have covered a half-acre of land on our property with wood chips to build the soil. The microbial life feeds constantly on the wood chips and the soil comes alive with activity and therefore feeds the fruit trees, berry bushes, berry vines, veggies, etc. It's pretty awesome! The last two years I've been seeking the Lord about creating on Earth what He had in Heaven! Two years!

I have been desiring this for so long! I've talked about it constantly with friends and family! I've started spreading wood chips and growing an abundant amount of food at our home...and NOW, I get to see how it truly is in Heaven!

WOW! I was more excited than my son is when we go to Subway! I said, "I want to see everything Lord! I desire to see what Eden is like!"

We started walking further down the golden pathway. We walked, I watched Jesus walk. It was truly something to behold. He has the posture still of a Jewish man that walked many miles across the Israeli landscape. The muscular lean build of a carpenter/home improvement contractor turned rabbi teacher! I was reading in between the lines as I beheld His posture. I could see all of the gospel stories totally with fresh perspective! I can see him making a whip and kicking out the thieves from the temple! I can see Him carrying a cross outside the city, and not being a coward in life. He was a man.

He was not a punk, sissy, limp hand, boy band Messiah. He was a man infused with Godly strength, bold compassion, and presence. He was man. He was all man. This man's manliness inspired every cell within me to be a Man! It was manliness defined by godliness alone. How can I describe this?

The manliness of Jesus reached deep into my soul and called me to be a whole man...a man of all character traits that cause all men to follow you! The God-ness before me had me trading all my manliness over to become nothing but a God-being only! He had me radiating desires to be manly, to be Godly, and to be Love's strongest example to all those I encounter!

I had this passage bubbling up within me. It's about the two men that took a walk out of Jerusalem down to a village called Emmaus. Jesus had just been crucified and now was resurrected! But these two men walking down the road had no idea...YET.

> **Luke 24:31-32 (KJV)**
> ³¹ **And their eyes were opened, and they knew him; and he vanished out of their sight.**
> ³² **And they said one to another, <u>Did not our heart burn within us, while he talked with us by the way</u>, and while he opened to us the scriptures?**

These two men were walking down the road and Jesus appeared and walked up to them and carried on a conversation as they walked down the path. Oh, I felt just like them! I was walking down a road/path with Jesus Himself!

When these two men on the road finally had their eyes opened, they knew it was Jesus! They said, "Did not our heart burn within us while he talked with us on the road!" Oh, my heart, my spirit, and my everything was burning as I walked and talked with the Alpha & Omega Himself!

Oh, when you walk with Jesus you feel FIRE BURNING within you to be all you were created to be!

He made me proud to follow! He made me want to go be the Jesus kind of manly in front of my wife Laura all the days of our life! He spread a flame inside of me to blaze this Jesus kind of manliness before my daughter Catalina all of her waking moments with me! Oh, I wanted this manliness to catch fire in my sons Daniel, Samuel, & Joseph! Oh, Jesus radiated all that I wanted to be!

Then I cried as I walked with Jesus. My eyes were on Him. He was the Son of Man.

I cried, when the Spirit said gently within me, "Brock, I'm showing you Me, because that's exactly the completeness that you were born again as…My image. You are My image bearer.

You carry a unique
***expression** of Me.*

Heaven Awaits Your Expression

You will radiate to the world the purest genuine expression of Me you were designed to give to the world. You were born to give the world one of the present-day examples of what a son of God expresses on the Earth in your day and age. Amen."

The Lord continued, "It is so. It is the plan of things. You are living and walking with Me right now on this golden way as I planned it before the foundations of the World. It is from the Father's bosom to your mother's bosom. Now sharing your heart with Me through the great Holy Spirit. We are one. We are all one in our inner man through the Spirit. We all walk within each other. We are one. Now, behold the inner sanctuary of the forests of Heaven."

Jesus was before me still in the same position as always to my front right. We were instantly there. We were within a vast forest. I was seeing dimly again. I knew we were there, but again; my mind was catching up with the Heavenly reality and light coming to me all around.

Jesus again, as was His custom, said, "Brock, what do you see?"

This time, I was going to put out wholehearted effort to see. I pushed my eye muscles to take in all the sights before me. The dimness was there. I kept letting the focus set in. I said, "Trees, I see lots and lots of trees. Huge trees! Those are the biggest trees I've ever seen in my life! I see the mountains! I see that mountain."

As soon as I saw that mountain, I seemed to have moved closer with Jesus. He wanted me to take in the full details of that mountain. All I could see now was that mountain. It was silhouetted with the horizon of the Father's glory on the opposite side of where we were standing. Even though we had no darkness or shade in Heaven, the brightness coming over the mountains top was beaming over the top with a measurable difference of Brightness! It was glory clouds pooling over like mists. It reminded me of the steam that spilled over a boiling pot while cooking. The glory dust clouds were steaming over and misting into the atmosphere.

Heaven Awaits Your Expression

I could make out just under the top of the silhouetted mountain peak there was a waterfall streaming out and flowing straight down from the top of the mountain all the way down to the ground. It seemed the mountain had a straight cliff all the way down to the ground where I was with Jesus. I noticed how the water was flowing straight from the top edge. Behind the waterfall was what I noticed to be shining gems, rubies, gold, & diamonds within the rock of the mountain.

"Brock, what do you see?" Jesus said again.

> *"Lord I see a beautiful mountain before us. I see the Father's light and glory beaming and cascading over the horizon of the mountain! I see a waterfall coming from the tip top of that mountain! But, the water! How is it doing that? Lord, the water is coming down in spirals. It's coming down like it's screwing in perfect spirals all the way down. How is that possible? Waterfalls on Earth fall straight down and kind of evaporate as they mist into the air...but this one is totally different."*

Jesus smiled a bit and said, "Brock, the water here reacted as soon as I looked in its direction. Here, everything reacts as soon as My face turns their direction. Do you remember the blessing the Hebrews would give in the Torah? Remember the phrase, "May His face shine upon you..." (Num 6:25) and you will understand the realities of that here in Heaven. Brock, everything I have said within the recorded Word of God carries Heavenly realities here. It's within the blueprints of all that I say. I am the same here as I am there and vice versa. The Spirit is in Me and He's in the water. On Earth I said that I was the Living Water. Here I am the Living water. The water sees me as its creator."

Jesus continued teaching me, "I am the full expression of every atom's individual self-image.

Heaven Awaits Your Expression

They bear My image and have the ability to give expression in their own individual way as any other created being in My creation. The water has the Living Water Spirit inside each atom and therefore lives, breathes, moves, and has its being by My life. All of life is connected by My Spirit. Every atom has particles of the light of My power. I uphold all things by the Word of My Power. (Heb 1:3)

I, by My Spirit, hold all of the created order in its created motion. I am that I am. My creation IS as I designed. It has been put into motion. It obeys. It does everything by design."

I then remembered how Jesus demonstrated this on the Earth by rebuking the wind and calming the sea. He walked on water and he changed water to wine. He multiplied bread and fish to thousand of people. When he needed money to pay taxes, he just went fishing and pulled the gold coin out of the fish's mouth!

Jesus paused. He turned to the water and then looked away to the right toward what looked like a way up to the top of the mountain. I noticed the water went back to flowing straight down! The water was living, breathing, and was privileged to carry God's Spirit like me! I am still puzzled how God in His infinite wisdom has ordered all His creation with individual respect and design. How wonderful and infinite is our God!

We started toward the path up the mountain. We didn't go far until we were instantly on top of the mountain! When I opened my eyes, I gasped. I was high overlooking much of Heaven! I froze. I decided to get my bearings about me. I wanted to orientate myself again. I was starting to get the hang of this. There weren't the same signs I looked for on Earth like where the Sun was rising or setting. There was no sun rising or falling here! First thing I did was open my eyes and see where the light was the brightest. That was easy!

You could first see the brightness of the light coming from the Father, then you could see in which direction the clouds were moving. The clouds, glory dust, color died star dust clouds all seemed to be flowing in a direction away from His throne.

New dust and glory were continually coming from the energy activity at the Father's person. You could stop what you were doing and listen. You could hear the activity from the throne from anywhere in Heaven. The thundering and lightning were constantly roaring. I took in everything, took a deep breath, and started to see. I opened my eyes with all my will. I projected my heart and soul to see all I could see! I looked toward the Throne!

What I saw was quite startling and is profoundly amazing. There was the throne so far out in the distance. It was still close…but still so far! His throne was atop a slowly ascending elevation. It was close to the way I remembered teachings of Jerusalem in the sense that any way you traveled into Jerusalem you had to travel up elevation. The City of David is on a mountain/hill. Jerusalem is also called Mount Zion. God's throne is on a mountain. The Heavenly Mt. Zion. It is glorious!

I started to see details. There were beautiful life, trees, and flowing greenery around the mountain. I knew within me that it was Eden as well. It seemed All of Heaven was Edenic. The whole planet was Eden! I saw those same rivers proceeding from God's mountain. That must be where the Tree of Life is! I remembered that there was a river that flowed out of the Throne area of the New Jerusalem, from the Tree of Life. It was called the Living Waters! I could see those rivers that flowed forth from the Mountain in each direction and flowed outwardly to all of the Planet Heaven! I counted four rivers. I was wondering if that one water source broke up into four rivers at first like that of Eden in Genesis?

Genesis 2:10

¹⁰ And a river went out of Eden to water the garden; and from thence it was parted, and became into <u>four heads.</u>

All the Springs of water came from God's throne!

Then I just took in the sight with amazement! I observed the massive cities with infrastructure all around the throne's massive temple area and those huge walls.

There was a huge temple around a massive portion of the Mountain, and then outside of the temple was a city! There were so much homes, buildings, and different cities! I was blown away!

I could see the cities from a better vantage point up here! I could see a lot of the city area. The city I saw earlier with the massive river going through it, with trees on the sides, and large streets on both sides was so clearly in front of me.

It was a sight to behold. Wow. I was trying my best to take in every detail I could. This time I had time to hear the Spirit bring up scriptures to illustrate what I was seeing. He brought these to my mind:

Revelations 22:1-2 (KJV)
> **1 And he shewed me a <u>pure river</u> of water of life, clear as crystal, <u>proceeding out of the throne of God</u> and of the Lamb.**
>
> **2 <u>In the midst of the street of it, and on either side of the river</u>, was there the tree of life, which bare twelve manner of fruits, and yielded her fruit every month: and the leaves of the tree were for the healing of the nations.**

Right there in Revelation 22! John was seeing what I was seeing. He talked about seeing the river, with the road on both sides, with fruit bearing trees on the banks.

Now, I don't think I saw the very beginning of the River of Life coming from the Throne where the Tree of Life was…but throughout the Heavenly Jerusalem, you could see the same setup of the river, trees, roads, and light!

I knew then that He said He goes and prepares a place for us. But this was on a massive scale! He prepares a place for every single one of His believers!! Holy Jesus, how great and majestic You are! I just started praising Him! Oh, that is amazing!

I started to realize that all of those cities were one large city, the Heavenly Jerusalem! This was Zion! This is what I've read about my whole life. It was all making more sense now! I could see the Walls that were described in the book of Revelation.

These were the Walls of the New Jerusalem that will be placed on the Earth! I could see how many jewels, gold, and artistry filled all of Heaven. Everything was made beyond beautiful!

I noticed something interesting. There were what looked like light towers throughout Heaven. Going out from the Throne, evenly spread out across the whole expanse of what I could see were these very thin lighthouses.

They were sort of like what we have on Earth- light houses. They had doors at the bottom and people could walk up and sight see from different heights. You could go to the very top platform and see the sights! Some were in the city and some were in the forests.

I knew inside that newcomers would go there immediately and take in the beauty of it all! I could see another peculiar detail. On the very top was a light reflecting the light from the Father out in every direction. It seemed to be a conductor of light. It seemed like it had a job to beam out the light in Heaven out in all directions and perhaps that was one of the ways the light was everywhere and there was no shade, shadow, or darkness? WOW.

It looked like the top had some kind of stone that was a light conductor. I'm not fully informed on this, but it was truly fascinating. It has been my discovery that light comes from the Father, reflects through the stars, these lighthouses, the trees, the ground, the water, etc. Basically, everything takes in the Father's light and is participating in giving it out as well.

The Spirit reminded me of the scripture:

Revelation 22:5 (KJV)

5 And there shall be <u>no night</u> there; and they <u>need no candle</u>, neither <u>light of the sun</u>; for the <u>Lord God giveth them light:</u> and they shall reign for ever and ever.

Revelation 21:23 (KJV)

23 And the city had <u>no need</u> of the sun, neither of the moon, to shine in it: for the <u>glory of God did lighten it</u>, and the Lamb is the light thereof.

Then, again, the Spirit used scripture to demonstrate to me how everything He does lines up with the Word of God! He brought this one to me next:

Revelation 21:10

10 And <u>he carried me away in the spirit to a great and high mountain,</u> and <u>shewed me that great city</u>, the holy Jerusalem, descending out of Heaven from God,

11 <u>Having the glory of God: and her light</u> was like unto a stone most precious, even like a jasper stone, clear as crystal;

12 And had a wall great and high, and had twelve gates, and at the gates twelve angels, and names written thereon, which are the names of the twelve tribes of the children of Israel:

13 On the east three gates; on the north three gates; on the south three gates; and on the west three gates.

14 And the wall of the city had twelve foundations, and in them the names of the twelve apostles of the Lamb.

15 And he that talked with me had a golden reed to measure the city, and the gates thereof, and the wall thereof.

16 And the city lieth foursquare, and the length is as large as the breadth: and he measured the city with the reed, twelve thousand furlongs. The length and the breadth and the height of it are equal.

17 And he measured the wall thereof, an hundred and forty and four cubits, according to the measure of a man, that is, of the angel.

18 And the building of the wall of it was of jasper: <u>and the city was pure gold, like unto clear glass.</u>

19 And the foundations of the wall of the city were garnished with all manner of precious stones. The first foundation was jasper; the second, sapphire; the third, a chalcedony; the fourth, an emerald;

> **20 The fifth, sardonyx; the sixth, sardius; the seventh, chrysolyte; the eighth, beryl; the ninth, a topaz; the tenth, a chrysoprasus; the eleventh, a jacinth; the twelfth, an amethyst.**
> **21 And the twelve gates were twelve pearls: every several gate was of <u>one pearl: and the street of the city was pure gold, as it were transparent glass.</u>**

I could sense that the Lord was doing exactly the same thing with me! I was caught up instantly to a great and high mountain, and He was shewing me that great city, the Holy Jerusalem! Wow!

I was seeing the city of gold! I was seeing transparent houses, beautiful libraries that were miles long, and what looked like schools! This place was amazing! I wanted to experience every part of Heaven!

Jesus gently willed me to turn around. "You will get to see that part of Heaven later, but now, I must show you what's before you now. What do you see?"

~

Again, I was snapped out of one moment into another.

"Lord, I see a pool of water. It's so gentle, pure, clean, and crystal clear. Lord, it's so serene. It's the water from the waterfall? It doesn't have the typical current of a waterfall. Hey, is this an infinity pool?"

Jesus nodded, "You can call it that if you choose." This is where I must baptize you. Come with me into the water."

Baptize me? Thoughts came rushing into me from the last water experience with Him. Oh, I knew this was happening. I found myself walking towards Him. I stepped my bare feet into the water. Yeah, it was alive and frizzing up and tickling every hair on my leg. It was massaging me and relaxing every part of me it touched. I found myself being completely at peace. At first, my heart rate seemed to go up a bit thinking that I was about to have another experience with Jesus.

Heaven Awaits Your Expression

The tears seemed to go into preparation. It's like my spirit, soul, and body were trained for every Jesus experience.

I peacefully stepped into the ripples coming out from where He stood smiling. Oh, He has a smile that says,

> *"You are the only created one I'm looking at right now. You are the only one I'm talking to. You are the only one my attention is on. You are the one I'm listening to. You are my Beloved. I am yours. We are in this moment together and I LOVE YOU so much!"*

I stepped to the spot beside Him where I knew inwardly, I was supposed to be. Jesus placed a hand over my heart. Jesus placed another hand behind my head. He stood with a new posture I saw for the first time. Now, I'm just looking at Him with trusting, blurry tear wet eyes. I'm watching Him. I'm taking on depths of revelation just watching Him move.

He stands up in what I'm thinking is the Kingliest Stance I've ever witnessed. He took on a Supreme King Posture. His face turned to a Judicial Righteous One. Creator of everything visible. He was THE ONE.

Ok, now the fear of God came back into my soul. Everything in me shut up and reverenced the moment. I was not to be out of line right here. His look told me that I am in a serious moment. I yielded with all my heart to the moment.

Jesus looked deeply into me. Oh, I was shaking again. I was trembling. Jesus began to speak,

> *"Brock, I am now taking away everything you thought you were. This is the moment I demonstrate who you truly are before my Father, Me, and the Spirit. Before the Father's Face, before all of Heaven's creation, before the angels*

Heaven Awaits Your Expression

present, I now take away from you your identity of your old life. You are no longer seen in my eyes as of the lineage of the Knight Family. You are no longer in remembrance of past failures. No longer will you or Me remember your past sin. You are free from sin. You are to die to yourself now. You are no longer Brock Edward Knight only. You are no longer your own. You are no longer anything but who I say you are and who I am within you! Now, you are crucified with me on my cross!"

He then took me by the head and began to take me forward to go face forward into the water. He began to say as my face merged into the water, *"Brock, you are now dying with me and dying unto yourself."*

I was fully under the water now. He held me under the water. I could feel the water tingling every part of me! I could hear Jesus speaking to me inside of me as I was under the water!

"You are buried with me. You are hidden in me. You are dead. Brock Knight is no more. I give you new eyes - My eyes! I give you new ears, mouth, nose, and a new body! Your mind is renewed now- I give you my mind! You have my body now!"

As He is saying all of this, the water is working in tandem with everything He says! The water was flowing into my eyes, flowing into my ears, flowing into my nose, mouth, and swirling all over my skin! Jesus held me there to soak in the moment. I could breathe underwater! That had me skip a beat! It truly is living water! You can't die in Heaven! You can breathe underwater! How amazing!

Jesus starts to pull me up. It was in slow motion! I came up out of the water and the light from the Father was directly in front of me! I came up with the sound of water, I heard angels singing around. I think there were angels singing in the largest choir EVER.

I just knew it was a choir. I didn't see them. I just heard the atmosphere of glory! I came from water into glorious light! It reminded me of the angels with the shepherds.

Luke 2:8-15 (KJV)

⁸ And there were in the same country shepherds abiding in the field, keeping watch over their flock by night.

⁹ And, lo, the angel of the Lord came upon them, and the glory of the Lord shone round about them: and they were sore afraid.

¹⁰ And the angel said unto them, Fear not: for, behold, I bring you good tidings of great joy, which shall be to all people.

¹¹ For unto you is born this day in the city of David a Saviour, which is Christ the Lord.

¹² And this shall be a sign unto you; Ye shall find the babe wrapped in swaddling clothes, lying in a manger.

¹³ And <u>suddenly there was with the angel a multitude of the heavenly host praising God</u>, and saying,

¹⁴ Glory to God in the highest, and on earth peace, good will toward men.

¹⁵ And it came to pass, as the angels were gone away from them into heaven...

The Father was beaming light right on to us! I felt like the light was many times brighter than it was when we started! It was so bright! It didn't affect my new eyes though! I just looked into the supernova of light and colors as Jesus lifted me up. All I could do was see colors untold and hear the most beautiful rejoicing and songs that were the perfect songs for the moment. I wish I could remember the songs. I can't remember one song though. Oh, I pray I remember at least one!

All the light and moment were transcended as Jesus turned me to look into His eyes.

He said, "Brock, this is truly what happens when one is born again and is baptized on Earth.

Heaven Awaits Your Expression

Once one believes and decides once and for all to repent and let Me be the King of their life, **they must be baptized in front of witnesses and declare that I'm their Lord.** There is so much power in that act. *Once a believer declares openly that I'm their Lord and repents, angels in Heaven sing and rejoice!* The old man passes away and Behold, all things are new, and all things are of Me and from Me!"

I was completely silent and taking it all in. I was not even breathing at all. Just all ears. The all too familiar scripture was coming to my mind:

Luke 15: 7 & 10

7 I say unto you, that likewise <u>joy shall be in Heaven</u> over one sinner that repenteth, more than over ninety and nine just persons, which need no repentance.

8 Either what woman having ten pieces of silver, if she lose one piece, doth not light a candle, and sweep the house, and seek diligently till she find it?

9 And when she hath found it, she calleth her friends and her neighbours together, saying, Rejoice with me; for I have found the piece which I had lost.

10 Likewise, I say unto you, <u>there is joy in the presence of the angels of God over one sinner that repenteth.</u>

Jesus continued,

"You are no longer Brock Knight. You are no longer seen from Heaven in Earthly statures. Brock Knight of the Knight Family heritage, from Tennessee, from the United States of America. Male. You are now a new man! You are made ONE with me! You are now a son of the Most High. You are now a citizen of Heaven. You now have freedom to be as I designed you to be. You are a Son. You are One with Me. You are no longer named and seen as Brock Knight only. You will carry the Name Above All Names- JESUS. You are a son from the lineage of Jesus, and you have access to come and learn from Me all you please. This is how I see you. I see you as a son of My Father and therefore a brother. You are of the tribe of Jesus. You are a priest under

Heaven Awaits Your Expression

the order of Jesus, within the line of Melchizedek. You're born again as a king under the King of Kings. You are a new creation. You now live IN ME. Everything I am, is what is now in you. It's my righteousness, my everything- in you. You live by faith. There's not male or female in this New Man. There's not Jew nor Greek, White or Black, it's just Me ALL IN ALL. Your Father sees you like Himself, carrying His image. Just like you see your children on Earth. You are born again complete and given the person of the Spirit. You are as I am on the Earth. Go as a Son of Jehovah and do as a Son does. Write what I teach you here and declare it to the World. Brock, you are to grow into Me. You are to become as I am. Our union is what matters. You can do what I do and say what I say. You have My body, My mind, My Spirit, My words, My Earth, My people, My angels, My Father, and My Heaven. You are Mine. I am Yours. Now, be who I have designed you to be. I have instructions for you to follow"

"Lord, this all seems beyond my experience so far as a disciple. It seems more than what most people understand and experience with the new birth and baptism?" I nervously needed edifying.

Jesus said strongly,

> *"I have said what I have said! You are given My name! Our Father calls all of His children by His name just as you call your children by your name. Your children are called Juniors. Men name their kids after their own names, right? I see all My children as My image bearers carrying My name. Satan sees what I see. It's time you and My church see themselves as they truly are. Are you not humans that carry God inside of you? Have not cultures past called men who were half human and half god demi-gods? Are you not demi-gods on the Earth if you have God inside of you? Does not my word say, "Ye are gods" and did not I quote that to the Scribes and Religious leaders? Don't I command my people to live*

godly? Brock, you have been born again and re-created as a literal Son of Almighty God. You are a human with a NEW SPIRIT. You have God in you. Listen, what makes a human alive? A human body without a spirit is dead. A human body with a spirit is alive. When one is born again, baptized in water, baptized in the Holy Spirit and therefore sealed by the Holy Spirit of God a MIRACLE HAS HAPPENED. A creative work by the Spirit has happened! You have been recreated, designed, & built by God to be a human with a Spirit that is one with the Godhead. You are now the seed of God. You are a Son! For all eternity you will be a Son! You bear the name of your Father! I AM the firstborn of all the Sons! I carry all the honors and all the authority as the firstborn within The Family. I have the full blessing and inheritance from the Father and am the Head of the Family. I'm the head of the Family Business - the Church. You are created to be like Me. You are to do the Father's Business as I did! Now, you must realize that you are a Son, your wife is a daughter, your children are sons and daughters as well. You each have assignments, placement, and destined purposes within the plan of My Kingdom. Do not shy away from the fact that you bear the Name of God. To those on Earth, you are Brock Knight. To me, you are My son. You are to learn to live as I do. I am God. You are to live Godly on Earth. Those who live Godly suffer persecution. People love you...until you begin to live truly one with Me! When you live as I do and do as I do, people will begin to react in evil ways. You will see My glory. Satan and his demonic horde will run from my power! They know you are with Me here...you are in the fight already. Now listen as I begin to lay out instructions for you to go forward."

I simply said all I could in response, "Lord, I am yours. Whatever you tell me to do, I will. I have you. You are my prize. I am satisfied with YOU. Please help me to follow every single detail you command."

CHAPTER 7

THE TREES IN EDEN

"It was as though every part of the creation I was looking at shared in reflecting the light of the Father!"

Next thing I knew we were off of the mountain and back down in the midst of the forest. This was the Ancient Eden as I understood. Jesus motioned to me to look around at all the trees. He didn't have to tell me twice! I was already flooded with details of the magnificence and magnitude of the trees around me. I mean, you had to see this to believe it! Some trees were probably a few thousand feet tall and who knows how wide!

They all seemed to wind inside and out and weave together through one another!

It was something amazing to behold! I saw all kinds of trees. Trees of color. Trees that seemed to not be wood. Some trees seem to be like precious metals and even glass or crystal. Who knows?

Heaven Awaits Your Expression

Again, what I was seeing was being processed within the little Earthly mind I possess. It was just some mind-blowing beauty for me to process. There were trees there that I knew we must not have on Earth!

Jesus signaled for me to come with Him. We appeared before a magnificent sight! I looked up.

The trees before me! I know these trees! These were none other than the Redwoods of Heaven. The original Redwoods! I thought out loud and said, "Sequoias...Redwoods!" He told me that they were originally created in Heaven and these in Heaven are from the very beginning. They were larger than skyscrapers in Downton cities! They were 2-3000 ft tall and so wide! He said that the ones we have down there in California are baby trees only. If it wasn't for the times of extinction disasters, they too would be this big!

As if that wasn't amazing enough, we were off to the next tree! The next tree was a tall tree as well, but only 1000 ft or so. It had no branches going up the trunk until the top. It had what looked like a ball of branches near the top and when Jesus looked up to the tree, it bent over and came all the way down to me and Jesus. The tree showed us its leaves and showed us its flower. The flower came up close to me and I got to take in all the details of the flower. It was a magnificent blue of some Heavenly sort and had a beautiful design of dots and lines that swirled down the cup of the flower where the pollen/nectar area was. The nectar/pollen tubes (the pistil, pollen tube, stigma, stamen, etc.) came out and showed that they were putting out a pollen and came into bloom right in front of me.

Jesus said, "Watch this"

He put His hand on the bulb (receptacle) of the flower and squeezed it. When He did, the flower burst out a fresh release of amazingness into my face! My face, eyes, mouth, brain, lungs, ears, and everything else in me lit up into a full complete awareness like I have never experienced! I felt more alive! I asked Jesus, "What was that? Wow!" Jesus told me that the flower gave out pure oxygen!

He explained to me how these trees were in abundance throughout the region around the garden of Eden on Earth.

Heaven Awaits Your Expression

They were even in abundance on the Earth after the Eden and up until the Flood. He said that it was because of this tree that the Earth could be filled with a fully potent measure of oxygen after the Fall. With the atmosphere like it was, these trees, other trees, and so forth, the animals and humans could live in almost perfect health, live extremely long, and even after sin they could live 900 years or more! It is something people can still use! He said that He never lets Satan fully destroy everything he desires to destroy on Earth. God has hidden this tree on the Earth. It's not for Satan or for His workers. It's for the sons of God. Perhaps He will show us where they are?

The next tree was an ancient fig tree. The tree was huge! It had long extended curved rigid arms going out approximately a hundred feet in both directions. The tree seemed to be nothing but lanky arms going outward and upward and had no leaves or fruit on it. I thought that was odd. Jesus told me it was a fig tree. The original fig tree that Adam ate from within the garden. He had the fig tree bring one of its massive arms close to us. It came right before me. Jesus began to look at the tree and the tree responded with an amazing display of worship to the Lord. The tree started to bud along the massive branches! It started to have green buds, then leaves folded out of the bud, and out came the beginning of a flower, fruit, and then all in one motion the life span of fruit bursting out into full ripeness happened all before my eyes. It turned into the most beautiful orange/gold mixed with a slight starburst design on the top of the fig.

The fig was beautiful and seemed to reflect light. It was perfection. It was a fruit that was pleasant to the eyes and desirable. Jesus took the fruit from the tree and handed it to me to eat. I was humbled. I was honored! I get to taste my very first fig fresh off of a tree in Heaven!

I have a few fig trees planted at my house and have talked to my wife about getting to eat our first figs from the trees one day! But now I get to try one in Heaven! I bit into the fruit and it was instantly fizzy, watery, and juicy. A mist was bursting out as I punctured the fruit. It was most certainly alive and as I was biting down, you could feel it bursting with flavor as soon as my mouth hit it! I bit and had an intensely pleasurable feeling all over! My eyes lit up and everything became extremely more crisp, clear, and brighter! I said, "Oh my! My eyes are completely new! Wow! I can see details extremely clearer! Wow!"

Heaven Awaits Your Expression

Jesus smiled and begin to tell me how that fig tree was designed for the health of humans. It was beneficial to maintain healthy eyes and to heal eyes. It would heal color blindness, heal cataracts, make eyes last longer, and cause eyesight to be perfect on Earth! He told me that Adam and Eve was clothed with the leaves from this fig tree. This is the genus of figs that they ate from. They were able to see for the 900 or so years after Eden because of eating these fruits.

Then I was like, "How is that possible?"

He asked me, "How long are people on Earth able to use their eyes presently?

I said, "Well, I guess 50, 60, 70, 80, 90, or so years" and I knew what He meant. He was clear now. Human's eyes start to dim with old age. They experience color blindness, wear glasses, contacts, have cataracts, etc. This fig tree could heal eyes! He said He took this tree out of service after Noah, and they have died away. The remnants are only partially potent. I started to wonder if the sons of God can have access to this tree on Earth? But as soon as I thought it, we were at another tree!

The next tree was a wild moving tree. It was moving back and forth when Jesus looked at it. It looked like a rock and roll singer with long hair rock'n and roll'n before Jesus and I. It had stringy branches with small leaves and flowers going down the whole branches. It was a lot like a Weeping Willow branch but stringier. Jesus said to the tree to come and it calmed down and came close. Jesus showed me the branches. He told me that this tree grew on mountains and high places where the wind was strong. It was used to being blown in the wind. It had flowers, roots, bark, etc. that all had potent qualities to heal cancer and other diseases. I was shocked. I was just speechless.

I did not have much questions at this point. He told me that this is available to the sons of God on the Earth and only the sons are allowed to release this onto the Earth. Wow. He showed me that we are supposed to use this in our hospitals/hospitality expressions, along with the pure oxygen flowers, and praying for the sick as well.

The next tree looked a lot like a huge pine tree. It looked a lot like the ones we have here in the Southeast, US. The loblolly pine to be exact. But this tree in a whole wasn't the center of Jesus' focus.

Heaven Awaits Your Expression

He had this moving alive black/brown substance above his hands. It looked like a movie with an alive alien gel moving around and expressing its life form. I asked Jesus what in the world that was, and He told me that it was the sap from that pine tree. He told me that this sap had the ability to increase sexual libido. Everything worked better down there... and in general, humans can be more fruitful and multiply. It was used to increase the fruitfulness on the Earth! God has created sex and made it to be amazing!

I think I blushed a bit. I was just in awe and blown away that Jesus was showing me this! He was talking about sex in Heaven!

Then He showed me a huge oak tree. It was huge. It was a grey looking metallic bark and it had huge roots. He told me to look. I looked up and the tree moved its branches down and picked us up seated within its branches up high enough to see over the other trees. Jesus asked me, "What do you see?" And I started to look. "I see more trees, a waterfall. It's not the same waterfall I saw last time. It's different."

Jesus confirmed and said, "Yes, we are in a different part of the forests of Heaven. What more do you see?" I told him that I could see that the water was flowing down but that I couldn't see where it was flowing to. I could only see it flowing downwardly. Jesus told me that it was actually flowing down under the trees!

Next, we were down lower, and I could see from the new vantage point where the water was entering down under ground. There was an underground river here! It was flowing down, and it was flowing just several feet underneath all the trees.

Maybe 15-20 feet below! Wow. Jesus then explained to me how that the roots of the Oak tree spread out wide and was the strongest roots within the infrastructure of Heaven's soil. He had the ends of the roots pop up way in the distance to show me how they were spread out very far and wide from where the trunk was. He said that all the other trees are intertwined and wrapped into the Oak tree roots. He said that they are like the big concrete pillars on a bridge. They hold all the other tree roots up over the running water. All the roots dangle down and drink freely into the living water below!

He brought to me the famous scripture in
Psalm 1:1-3:
> **1 Blessed is the man that walketh not in the counsel of the ungodly, nor standeth in the way of sinners, nor sitteth in the seat of the scornful.**
>
> **2 But his delight is in the law of the Lord; and in his law doth he meditate day and night.**
>
> **3 And he shall be like a tree planted by the rivers of water, that bringeth forth his fruit in his season; his leaf also shall not wither; and whatsoever he doeth shall prosper.**

He taught me that it's the same on Earth. Oak trees are great trees that build a strong infrastructure in the soil for forests!

Jesus explained to me how that every animal in Heaven has exactly what it needs from the plant life. Every single created thing had what it needed from the other plant life. Humans as well. Humans have everything they need to live eternally whole and healthy lives in Heaven. That's how God created the Earth originally. It had everything we needed to live long healthy immortal lives. Satan has done all he can to destroy the beneficial plants and life on Earth.

Next, we were beside a beautiful stream. I knew, instantly, that we were downstream from the deep forest I had originally visited. We were still in the forest. It was still full of trees. I looked around and still was stuck on the fact that we were surrounded by the largest trees I've ever seen, under a huge canopy of trees, and these trees were thick- and yet there was no shade. Typically, in a forest you are living in some shade, some relevant darkness is present within the thick forested areas. Right? This goes against all my experience! I thought through my many days out in the woods. Now, I could remember that yes, there was light in the woods under the thick trees in the daytime hours. Yet, there was a lot of shade! But not here! I was in complete awe.

Heaven Awaits Your Expression

I studied the trees and noticed that they seemed to reflect light! Each trunk, branch, leaf, etc. all seem to be reflective.

It was as though every part of the creation I was looking at shared in reflecting the light of the Father!

I looked at the ground around me. I saw amazing ferns, amazing flowers in the middle of the forest, and grasses too! I was confused when I saw fruit bearing bushes, vines, and trees everywhere! I was all too familiar with fruit bearing trees, bushes, & vines on my farm needed a lot of sun! Typically, they didn't do too well under a canopy of trees! But here it was totally thriving!

I noticed the stream of water. It was the size of a small creek. It was absolutely portrait worthy! I could see so clearly through the water! "Whoa! Jesus, that is amazing! Wow!" I found myself talking out loud as I was noticing all the diamonds, gems, quarts, emeralds, rubies, etc. at the floor of the stream. There were beautiful stones everywhere! The big rocks on the side of the creek were pretty as well. The one I set my eyes on had glitter throughout all of it! It hummed with an energy and almost to a familiar song. I realized that Jesus was near-by, so maybe that's why it was humming so clearly. This was so much to take in!

I kept staring at the creek bed. All of those precious metals just laying around naturally in the water! I look on the banks of the water way and sure enough, there were emeralds and all the mixture of precious metals and stones that you could imagine. It was way more than what we are familiar with on Earth. There were many beautiful chunks of shiny beautiful stones. Down to the size of sand and up to gravel size. It was the soil. The soil wasn't as we know it here. There was not topsoil made up of layers and layers of dead material! Nothing died in Heaven! This was the soil! It was the original ingredients from the beginning! The trees fed from the life and energy coming from God Himself! They didn't need to feed from the death of other created beings like they do on Earth now after the Fall of Humans. They were not subject to the futility and subjection of Death and Sin! Oh wow! The design and mind of our God is worthy to be praised!

I looked back and Jesus after I felt inside that He was about to say something.

I just instinctively stood up and listened before I even heard a word. Wow. I thought to myself. You're getting the hang of this- this is amazing!

Jesus looked all around and then at the stones in the water. He explained, "Brock, I originally created all of Earth like this. There were stones and beautiful rubies in the water and in the soil. There still is actually in some places. But man has mined and scavenged the Earth to profit from my precious stones. There used to be diamonds, emeralds, rubies, etc. just like this all through the streams in the forests on Earth. Not anymore."

I asked Him, "What about the water under the forest like we saw earlier?"

He smiled, "If you remember in the book of Genesis, it shows how there were rivers flowing through Eden. It mentions even the gold and pretty stones that were found in the waters, remember?"

Wow! I remembered instantly:

Genesis 2:10-14
> **10 And a river went out of Eden to water the garden; and from thence it was parted, and became into four heads.**
> **11 The name of the first is Pison: that is it which compasseth the whole land of Havilah, <u>where there is gold</u>;**
> **12 And the gold of that land is good: there is <u>bdellium and the onyx stone</u>.**
> **13 And the name of the second river is Gihon: the same is it that compasseth the whole land of Ethiopia.**
> **14 And the name of the third river is Hiddekel: that is it which goeth toward the east of Assyria. And the fourth river is Euphrates.**

Jesus kept explaining, "As to your question on the water underneath the forest.

Remember in Genesis, when it describes the garden, it says that the water came up from the soil. A mist came up and watered all the trees, remember?"

Then I felt the scripture come through:

Genesis 2:5-6:
5 And every plant of the field before it was in the Earth, and every herb of the field before it grew: for the Lord God had <u>not caused it to rain upon the Earth</u>, and there was not a man to till the ground.
6 But there <u>went up a mist</u> from the Earth, and <u>watered the whole face of the ground.</u>

Then Jesus continued on, "Brock, right now, the water is in the Earth still. Water drains through the soil and returns to the aquifers down below. Much has changed since the Fall of Adam. Much of the systems are still in effect but tainted and all of the forests of Earth struggle day by day to do as they were commanded to do in the beginning.

To this very day, the best places on Earth to be are in the forests. That's why I love it here. It's the place where you find the most obedience on the Earth. The trees, the plants, the animals, the birds, the soil, and even the air are all striving to obey My original commands! I love it when you or My people visit with Me and seek Me out in the woods as you call it. My presence, My peace, and My voice are always more welcomed in a place full of obedience. Sometimes you can hear me better in the woods than in a building full of believers. One is full of obedience, and the other is in rebellion too often."

I could feel the heart of Jesus towards his Bride. He wasn't disgusted with His Church though. However, His definition of those in the Church is different than what we typically hear. He's not referring to the population of the Earth that identifies as a "Christian" or even those who say they believe. He's referring to those humans in which the Spirit of God dwells. Those who are

His disciples on the Earth. Those who are worshipping Him in spirit and in truth. This much was clear as I heard Him speak.

His heart toward those who were truly abiding in the vine was becoming apparent. It was like how a Father talks about a toddler son who keeps refusing to use the potty. He knows all too well that they will grow up and use the restroom properly. However, it's not like the Father lets the child stay in that same stage of life forever. Have you seen a 30-year-old man wearing diapers and crying to their mom when they have a "poopy?" Likewise, He makes SURE His sons grow up and do as is expected and what is right! Oh, the love in the heart of Jesus for His people. I also noticed the stern seriousness in His voice. He would not rest until His people were obedient and mature sons of God! He was SERIOUS about the children of God growing up into mature and strong sons!

CHAPTER 8

THE ANIMALS IN HEAVEN

"For some reason, this small act had me quivering with the all-consuming greatness and omniscience of Our Maker!"

Jesus then pulled me out of my thinking and nudged me inside to look across the stream. Standing in the distance not too far away was a beautiful deer! No antlers. Just a beautiful doe, with spots. Maybe a mixed breed of a whitetail and some other. Oh, who knows! She was beautiful.

It startled me! I was taken back! What in the world!!!! The deer spoke to me inside! Not with words, but I knew what it was saying. Oh, how do I explain this? She wanted me to look into her eyes! I nudged Jesus within me and instantly knew that He was in on this. So, I looked at the eye that was closest to me on the deer!

It was, of course, a feature of my eyes that I was inexperienced with. I guess my Heavenly eyes come with a zoom function too! OOOH WOW! I was looking up close to the eye of this deer! You can guess what I saw! The same beautiful star bright identity comparable to that of the angel, Jesus, the star, the Father, our own eyes on Earth, and now this beautiful deer! This had me shaking with wonder.

Heaven Awaits Your Expression

I didn't know what to do. What do you say? For some reason, this small act had me quivering with the all-consuming greatness and omniscience of Our Maker! The thought and detail He even gives to the animals had me in a state of dumbfounded reverence.

Next, my attention was placed on the water flowing down the curve of the stream. I was studying how the water connected with the rock. I was seeing how the water was dancing and swirling and in an electric expression to the presence of Jesus and myself.

Jesus told me to walk into the stream. Before I could consciously make myself do that, I realized I was already doing it! I was standing in the water. I laughed a bit and enjoyed the sense of humor of Jesus. I was looking back at the water and it was dancing, shooting up streams of water as you see in a fountain, and it was moving as though some frequency or electric pulse was attached to it. I looked at Jesus and He purposefully wasn't looking at the water. I was like, "Um, you're not looking this direction?" At first, I was a bit thrown off. But then, inside, I felt the gentle light of the Spirit point out a little nugget I missed. I was in the water, and I was just looking at the water…not Jesus! The water was dancing because I was there, and I was looking at it! Whaaaaaaaaat????

Jesus was then talking to me inside taking advantage of this lesson in the water. "You see Brock, the water celebrates every son, a lot like they do me when I look at them. They know your standing within this kingdom. You are the ones on Earth who represent Me and bear My position as a son. They recognize the delegated authority I've given to other sons. Any believer who was to walk where you are would experience the same exact thing!"

He brought this scripture to my mind:

Matthew 11:11

11 Verily I say unto you, Among them that are born of women there hath not risen a greater than John the Baptist: notwithstanding <u>he that is least in the kingdom of Heaven is greater than he.</u>

Jesus further taught me using that scripture, that even the least in the Kingdom of Heaven is greater that John the Baptist and all the former prophets! To be born again and be adopted as a son in His Kingdom was to be in a position of great importance. Being in the position of a son, comes with the anointing that comes with the position. Just as those in great positions in times past (prophets, kings, & priests) were anointed with oil, so too the sons of God are anointed into the position of a son, and they receive the greatest of honors. They receive greater than all of those prophets, kings, & priests in the Old Covenant.

Jesus said, "The sons in My family receive the creation of a new spirit within them and the infilling of the Person of the Spirit of God. When one is born again into a new creation, they are made one with me and they are anointed into the position of a son - just like Me!

The scriptures started flooding into me. I saw Samuel, David, Samson, prophets, priests, and kings alike having the horn of oil poured on them. I saw the Spirit of God come upon them because of the position they held:

1 Samuel 10:1 & 10:6-7 (example of Saul)

> **1 Then Samuel took a vial of oil, and poured it upon his head, and kissed him, and said, Is it not because the Lord hath <u>anointed thee</u> to be captain over his inheritance?**
>
> **6 And <u>the Spirit of the Lord will come upon thee</u>, and thou shalt prophesy with them, and shalt be <u>turned into another man</u>.**
>
> **7 And let it be, when these signs are come unto thee, that thou do as occasion serve thee; for God is with thee.**

1 Samuel 16:13 (example of David)

> **13 Then Samuel took the horn of oil, and <u>anointed him</u> in the midst of his brethren: and <u>the Spirit of the Lord came upon David</u> from that day forward.**

Jesus explained to me that these men (Saul & David) were anointed to be kings, in that position.

Because of their position, the Spirit of the Lord would come upon them when needed. That was the case for John the Baptist and all of the saints before Christ's crucifixion and resurrection.

Now, let's look at what He said in Nazareth:

Luke 4:17-19 (example of Jesus)

17 And there was delivered unto him (Jesus) the book of the prophet Esaias. And when he (Jesus) had opened the book, he found the place where it was written,

18 The Spirit of the Lord is upon me, <u>because he hath anointed me</u> to preach the gospel to the poor; <u>he hath sent me</u> to heal the brokenhearted, to preach deliverance to the captives, and recovering of sight to the blind, to set at liberty them that are bruised,

19 To preach the acceptable year of the Lord.

And Jesus continues on with His lesson, "You see, the Spirit of the Lord came upon Me BECAUSE I was anointed to preach. I was positioned in the Kingdom of Heaven as a son of God. That's the position I was anointed unto. I was the Christ, the Messiah, the first Son of God in the Kingdom of Heaven walking as the Son of Man. The first Son among a whole new race of Sons adopted into this family. That was my position. Because I was a son, the Spirit of My Father dwelt inside of Me. I walked in the fullness of the Spirit. I was fully and completely submitted and yielded to do as My Father pleases. Therefore, anytime I went about doing good the Spirit's power came upon Me, through Me, and out of Me to all those I touched! It's the same with every son of God alive on the Earth today. Each one has My Spirit and they are all anointed as sons of God and have My Spirit to do My great commission on the Earth."

I was eating every single word He said! I was like the prophet Ezekiel and the Apostle John who were told to eat the scrolls they were given.

I felt like it was going down like honey and I was being transformed and changed from glory to glory with every word He spoke!

Heaven Awaits Your Expression

I was taking on new expressions of God imprinted within my psyche. I felt so empowered and grateful to be one of the sons of God!

Jesus pointed down the stream. I looked and standing right there, looking right at me with eyes like I've never seen! It was the largest lion I've ever seen. It was a male lion. The lion had the look of the lion in Narnia! It had the largest and the most powerful looking mane! It was a scary and fearful and yet majestic sight to see! He was just jaw dropping amazing to look at. There were no scars on him though. I was used to seeing lions on documentaries that have scars from fights and rough mains. Most of what I expected in a lion was them looking at me and being hungry. I expected inside the lion's tongue to go around its mouth and drool at the sight of me.

Instead, I locked eyes with this big guy, and he said to me, "No Brock, I'm not a meat-eater as you suppose. I have fruit here to eat that satisfy me with the passion to hunt as I was created. I don't have to eat here. I enjoy my responsibilities here and I get to teach children about the animals here. Children actually love me here, and parents trust their kids with me alone! I'm instructed to take you to the bluffs down the stream. Come with me!"

It was all happening so quick. I seem to be traveling with the lion instantly to the bluff.

It's amazing how you can travel from one place to another so fast in Heaven. It seems you can travel at the speed of thought. You can fly. You can breathe under water. You can't die here. All things were possible here. So, take your pick! If you want to jump out of a 3,000 foot tree, you could! It is simply mind blowing.

Here I was standing beside, well, it seemed like I was beneath the large lion. This guy stood about 10 feet or so. I couldn't believe how big this guy was.

I hear the old gentle giant say to me, "I've been here since before the Earth was formed. I was copied to make the beasts on your planet. They were more like me in the beginning. We were not the biggest at first. We were like the little house cats you humans keep as pets.

Heaven Awaits Your Expression

We were small compared to those guys over there…when they were at the top of the food chain down there. Here, we don't eat one another. We don't need to. We have jobs and enjoy obeying our King and providing our service to all those who live here! Those who live here keep us entertained and we do them as well…"

I was losing him. I couldn't even hear anything else the large lion was saying due to the amazing sight before me! I could not believe my eyes! I couldn't keep in the shock and excitement all together! I could sense the joy of Jesus inside of me and the amusement of the lion as well. Standing all around down in the prairies below the bluff and as far as I could see were…none other…than…dinosaurs!

Yup. Dinosaurs.

Sure was! There were dinosaurs and big huge beasts that I've never seen in the *Jurassic Park* movies! There were large dinosaurs everywhere! Some were drinking water, some were standing underneath waterfalls, some were eating from tall trees, some were playing with others, it was the whole scene you would see from a dinosaur movie!

I immediately asked Jesus curiously about the one dinosaur I've always loved - the T-Rex! Oh yes! I wanted to know if the T-Rex would eat the other dinosaurs in Heaven! Just as I asked, I knew the answer! He already told me. But oh, was my Earthly information interfering with this Heavenly knowledge!

He told me that the T-rex has all its needs in Heaven! It does have its thrill of a hunt in Heaven! It got that from some big, huge fruits that grow on certain trees. It gives off a scent when it fruits and the T-Rex has to smell, hunt, and pursue the tree and it enjoys biting into the fleshy fruit. The T-Rex has all it needs here! I was simply in a state of not asking any more questions! I thought that was the most amazing discovery EVER! I couldn't wait to tell my son Daniel! He would love that neat detail.

I thought to myself, "How did the deer and the lion just speak to me? Lord?"

Jesus graciously responded, "Brock, the same Spirit in you and I is within both the deer and the lion.

You remember how I used the donkey to speak? You remember in the garden how the serpent spoke? It's the same. My Spirit is within the animals here. They can speak spirit to spirit. You'll get used to it. The kids love it! Kids here have the best life you could ever imagine! I'll show you later. Let's continue."

I was lost in amazement and just took in all the details. You know, I could write a whole book just on the animals, dinosaurs, trees, and plant life I saw there. There's not enough time and space to accomplish that. You will just get to do all of that adventuring once you arrive! What a day that will be!

Heaven Awaits Your Expression

CHAPTER 9

BRICKS OF GOLD

"I felt the brick move and ripple close to what I would see in a pond as you skip a rock. It rippled back and forth from hand to hand."

Jesus then asked me, "Where would you like to go now?"

I thought quickly, "Lord, I just want to go wherever you want me to. Anywhere!"

Jesus said, "Come, let's go to the street...here, now, what do you see"

I answered, "I see gold. This is a road? The gold bricks, they seem to be so thick. They're not the same as bricks on the Earth. These are solid gold, and they go down so deep."

I reached down and felt the brick. It wasn't attached. The brick was able to be moved. I felt for the edges and wedged my finger between the brick and the brick next to it. I started to pull up. My mind told me that it would be attached or too heavy, but I was wrong. It pulled up with a shocking ease. The weight was not at all what I was expecting. I'm guessing that a block of gold would be extremely heavy on Earth. This was not. The block looked approximately 8-9 inches long, 5-6 inches wide, and somewhere close to 2 feet thick/high. Wow. I held it up into my hands and thought, "This is just one of the bricks."

Heaven Awaits Your Expression

I held the 2 feet long thick solid gold brick in my arms without a strain! I looked at it. I saw it wasn't showing imperfections.

It wasn't showing rot, or the typical stains we would see on Earth. It had a musical instrument vibe to it. It seemed to be of the quality and the making like unto brass instruments. It was like that of a trombone, trumpet, and other instruments- but it was solid gold. It was made for vibration. It seemed like I could play music on this block of gold.

How is this gold block so pristine? How is it so perfect? It is walked upon. It is a part of the street! That's the most trampled part, the most common part of Heaven I'd imagine. Perhaps restrooms are more common? I mean, how is this so clean and beautiful?

"Brock." Jesus was calling me. I was instantly caught out of my thoughts and I was turning, seeing the surrounding buildings, city, or neighborhood. I couldn't make much observations of the city yet, but I registered in my mind they were in the background. I turned, saw the brown, original, human hair of Jesus. I instantly felt the bond of love that comes only from being in the presence of Jesus. Slow motion, I was in the moment again.

Jesus was beside me, and now before me. Jesus was there. Oh, my soul! Oh, my knees must keep me standing! I just want to talk to Him. Please let me have strength to walk with Him! I was next looking into His eyes. I was pulled in. I was absorbed into those life-giving eyes. I could see again the universe of life being held by the authority of His words. I can see the color, the light of what looked like torches. That's what I knew to be star light glory, the glory of His eyes. Oh, I want to stare into His eyes forever. I felt so accepted. Oh, I am home here. He was speaking to me and I must listen. His eyes were alluding to me that I must listen to what He is starting to say.

I paused. I breathed. I cried.

"Brock, I want to you look at that brick of Gold." Jesus started.

I looked back down instantly without a thought. I instantly wondered how does that work? How can He say something, and I am instantly springing into action? I did it. Yet, I did it without thought. I instantly looked at the gold without willing to. Did Jesus make me look at it?

Heaven Awaits Your Expression

This is so beyond me. How does that work? One moment I'm crying and just overwhelmed by Beauty Himself. The eyes of Wonder. The eyes had me completely self-aware that I'm before my Maker and He is accepting me and talking to me. For me to be within that proximity of Jesus Himself has me feeling the glorious miracle of the moment. I want to stop and take in all the details and not let one particle before me slip. I want to study his hair! I want to study His features. I want to gaze into His eyes until I remember every color, each star like activity blazing within Him, and never ever forget it.

But here I was looking at the gold. Like that. Just a quick instant. Quick as a thought. I was snapped out of my adoration to this gold brick. I was still holding it in my arms like I would hold a baby. It was there. I had 100% forgot about it. I forgot ALL once I saw His eyes. But here I am. I'm looking at a gold brick.

Jesus goes on,

"Listen, that brick was designed not to be common as you think. You must take a concept in right now before you go on. Nothing here is common. Not one atom on this planet as you would call it has commonality as you have thought. Here, all things are seen and understood by the glory from which they were created. Each brick is honored, respected, and given individual purpose. That brick has been giving off it's designed praise to the Father for eternity. You can feel its expression as you hold it. Look at the brick and say, 'Thank you'".

I did, without thinking, and said, "Thank you".

I felt the brick move and ripple close to what I would see in a pond as you skip a rock. It rippled back and forth from hand to hand. I trembled. I had no idea that even this brick was alive. What made it move like this?

Jesus knowing my thoughts, "Brock, that brick is made of the same building blocks of life you are. That gold is made of what you would call atoms, cells, or mass. It is a combination of a large number of smaller nucleuses combined into this object you hold. Watch this."

Jesus holds out His hand and does a wave of His hand. He does what I would guess a King would do.

One who is used to giving commands. Jesus moved His left hand out, and then slightly jerked his Hand over to the left. It was as If he was commanding the gold.

The gold was moving in my hands.

The gold flattened and stretched out long ways. Before my eyes a sword was forming. It turned into a majestic sword. It was a short sword. It was round handled. Had a guard between the handle and the blade. The blade went out close to 2 feet. The blade was gold, it was all gold! I stood there momentarily stunned. There was nothing to say! I just stared at the sword. I was holding it. There were details I was looking at that had me in awe.

The handle had grips. I wondered if the grips were made to fit my hand. Then I realized that I was in Heaven. That was my knowing. This knowing ability was the coolest thing ever!

I instinctively asked, "Can I hold it? Oh, and I'm not trained in swords Lord. I have watched lots of movies and videos though. Let's see what I know."

Why was I talking that way? I seemed giddy and nervous like a little school kid at show and tell. I felt so child-like like around Jesus sometimes. Was I truly feeling like a kid talking with a Father? Oh, it's hard to explain. I just don't know how to explain the feeling of being so completely loved, accepted, and free to express you're whole being to someone. It would have to be compared to how a young kid can act before a loving parent. Perhaps they are so free and carefree with their love.

They have no concept of their parent not loving them or accepting them. They are loud, playful, and run up to their parents and interrupt anything, completely oblivious of adult needs and obligations. I guess it's close to that.

I am standing here in Heaven as a full adult in my 30's and literally feeling so one with Jesus and free that I'm operating in His presence as a toddler. Oh the experience is just wonderful and different from our adult experiences on Earth. Oh, that the church would grasp the true love of Christ on the Earth!

Heaven Awaits Your Expression

If those within the family of God could learn to love one another so purely that we could all be wholly free, accepted, honored, respected, and loved without any fear of judgement. If we could just feel free to be loved and not be scared by each other's insecurities, judgements, and expectations. If we could just open our arms and love each other like a parent loves a toddler. Like parents unconditionally love their kids. We would see glory on Earth like waters cover the sea! We ought to love as He has loved us! We should unconditionally love even our neighbors! We would look not only at the interest of ourselves, but also on the interests of others.

I thought back to the teachings of Jesus where He told his disciples to have child-like faith and humility. Oh, this was taking on a whole new understanding within me now!

Jesus nodded approvingly.

I started back with the sword again. I changed the positions of my hands. I placed one hand onto the grip. I'm right-handed, so I wrapped my right hand onto the handle, and it felt like I became a part of the sword! I felt signals connecting my skin to the handle. I instinctively did what I saw in movies or videos. I held my index finger out and placed the sword over my finger in the center of the sword, near the guard. I wanted to see if the sword balanced. Why? I have no idea! I thought that's what you do with a sword. Seemed proper for characters in movies! I did. Guess what. The sword was perfectly balanced. Not a budge.

I realized that I could've not been in the center! How would I know what the center of a sword was? I tried the same thing at a different place. I moved more to the side of the guard where the blade was. I did the same thing from that side. It was perfectly balanced. Hmmmm. I tried another spot down the blade. It was balanced. Whoa. I looked at Jesus puzzled.

He smiled, "Brock, you need to know. Everything within you communicates with the sword. You were looking for balance, were you not?"

I said, "Yes" nodding affirmingly.

Jesus began to teach,"Well, anything you look for, anything you will, and anything you desire will come out through the sword.

Heaven Awaits Your Expression

Remember, everything it's made of is the same material you are made from. I am its creator. My Spirit holds the sword together as He holds you together. You must understand that in My Creation all things are held together by Me. I have spoken. My words put the activity of every cell together. Every small particle is moving within the atoms as I have spoken. The elements in every cell come from me. Remember how I took of the ribs of Adam and created another? I used what I created in Adam and propagated another."

Jesus continued, "That's how I created Adam. I took of me. I am the stock. I am the stock genes, the atom's origin. I have taken of Myself and copied the atoms from myself and have created all things. I just form the atoms into each and every object you can see with your eyes and those parts of creation that you can't see. Truly, you can see all things. You lack the experience son. I'll teach you one day to see all things visible and invisible. My sons are created after my image and have the ability to see even the smallest invisible created order. My invisible creatures are just as much my creation as the whole individual it makes up."

At this point, I had recalled all of my biology and science classes, the books I had personally read, and information from the videos over the years all at once. I was having confirmation of everything he was saying simultaneously.

He kept teaching, "Let's think of it as comparable to how a universe is made up of galaxies. The galaxies are made up of systems that orbit within a designed order to function accordingly. You know of your galaxy. You have seen pictures. Remember, the atoms and smallest of quantum individuals are systems that have moving parts working together as one. They each have a designed order. My Spirit is the life that holds all systems together and moving. Brock, all things, all systems, all life within the created order of God's expanse is connected. The air you see on Earth is thick with particles, atoms, individuals moving around doing as they were created to. Think about water.

Water has what your scientists have documented to be a multitude of countless life forms swimming around.

Heaven Awaits Your Expression

The mass of atoms that make up what you call water is just as condensed in the air as well. The air is the anthesis of water. The air is thick with atoms and fully connected just as the water. The Earth, the soil, the rock, etc. is the same. Everything you can see and not see on Earth is completely connected and densely packed with life. It is just different densities. You can move your hand through water and feel it. You can move your hand through soil and feel it. You can move your hand through the air and feel it. Now, do you see what I'm saying?"

I replied enthusiastically, "Oh yes. This is amazing. Please keep going. I'm fully following you." I was standing there, with a sword in my right hand, listening to Jesus teach me Biology, Physics, and I guess Quantum Physics. I loved every second of this!

Jesus continued on,

"Brock, you must realize that here in Heaven, everything is fully connected, fully one, and fully alive. On Earth, everything is fully connected, struggling to be one, and struggling to live. Earth was created exactly like you are experiencing here in Heaven. I created Earth as a copy of what I have here. Eden was the re-creation of Heaven on Earth. It was the incubator and weaning of a newborn son on the Earth. I taught him every single truth I'm teaching you. Adam was the most educated man in the history of your kind. Still is. He was educated fully of Heaven and Earth. He knew the millions of years' worth of knowledge, experience, observation, and insight. Adam observed, listened to me, and talked to the animals. Adam and I discussed each animal. We talked of the purpose, the jobs, the benefits, and the design of each animal, each plant, the air, the soil, and the water. Adam was thoroughly trained by Me. Now, I'm going to do the same with you. I AM the One who trains, teaches, and instructs. I am the Great Teacher."

Jesus kept teaching,

"Brock, we don't need toilets in Heaven. We don't have death here. We don't have waste. We don't pee and we don't poop.

Here, the nutrition from anything we eat is absorbed completely into the body.

Heaven Awaits Your Expression

We enjoy the pleasure of the food, but we don't have to digest and push out waste in any way. On top of that, you should know that there is nothing here that isn't respected and honored as an original. Each blade of grass, flower, tree, angel, cloud, piece of gold, precious metal, mineral, and atom is made of me, by me, and for me. Each order of my creation is designed to give expression as needed within my kingdom realm. You are holding a brick of gold. Is it a brick of gold or a sword? You answer that."

"Ummm, it's ummm" and yeah, that's my response. It was a trick question that was mind boggling. "Well, it's gold. It's designed for the expression you designed it for. It is a rare metal on the Earth. It's rare and therefore holy. There's none like it. There's none like you Lord! You are more than rare. You are The One. I AM. There is none beside you, behind you, or in existence. You are. You Is. You Will be. You are the precious of all metals. So, I guess this gold, in whatever form you tell it to be in, is giving off the expression of its Creator. It's praising and shouting out to all the inhabitants of Heaven that You are the most beautiful, radiant, and rare one in all existence! This gold shouts its own God given expressive worship to You and to others! Oh, that is amazing! This gold is living a life of purpose just as I am! Oh, I'll never look at gold the same! Each atom within each and every object I see is made to give off the vibrations of praise and worship!"

I cried. I lifted my hands. I was swept up into an overcoming worship that had me holding up the sword in worship.

Jesus lifted His hands.

All of Heaven shook. I felt the gold beneath me on the street vibrating in response. The Earth. What do I call it here? The ground? The ground was shaking!

The buildings hummed around me with an instrumental vibration. It was as if someone took a xylophone wooden mallet and began to strike each house to give off a sound. The hum was instantly a gorgeous chord that had me weeping. Oh, I wish we could make this sound on Earth! Oh, it has swept my soul right out of my body! I am swept up into adoration!

Heaven Awaits Your Expression

Oh, I'm pouring out! I'm gushing out! I noticed that people in the distance down the street had all stopped and turned their bodies toward the Father's light, their hands raised. I could perceive children on the street caught up into the worship. Small children too! I couldn't see them at first, but now I caught a glimpse of my surroundings just as I was swept away into this glorious exaltation!

I felt Jesus inside move upon me to understand the moment. Jesus had called all of Heaven into assembly to worship the Father! I was to turn around and join in. Heck, I thought I was already in! But then I turned, and I wept aloud and screamed with a guttural primate sound that I've never heard come out of me. I cried in utter shock and awe. I screamed. I straight up lost it. I can't express how my whole being came alive. My members each took a voice of their own and we all released what was ordered of me by the Throne in this unction of worship to the Father.

I was hearing all. I was hearing ALL. I was hearing ALL OF CREATION. I was hearing Jesus sing! Oh, I heard Him sing and it was entirely beautiful and frightening! It was vibrating so much that my being was just moving in and out and all over.

I felt like a character in a cartoon when they were hit with a gong or cymbal and their whole being moved in and out in vibration. I was swept up and vibrated and shook and screamed and cried and pushed out my being to the Father!

I was in complete connection with the gold, with the atmosphere, with Jesus, in the Spirit, and joining in with the hosts of Heaven! I looked at the Father's color exploding from His person! The Glory dust clouds rolled out like atomic clouds and lightning was spraying in all directions, with what felt like thundering but more like planet vibrations. It had all of me in tune. I was hearing not just with ears. I was hearing through ALL of whom I was connected. I was hearing from others. The gold? The other people praising with me? I willed to see who.

Heaven Awaits Your Expression

I looked just out from the throne with some kind of peripheral vision. I saw people in the sky singing! Ok, those most be angels. But it sure looked like people too.

I saw people in the sky worshipping. Angels and people. I think it was both. Could they fly? How did they get to the sky? Oh wow. They were spread out wide. Hands out wide and legs out wide giving their every bit of expression of praise to the Father!

I heard a leading voice inside of me, "Holy…HOOOOOLLLYYYY."

I instantly without thought was focused in on the throne. I was swept up and swept away. I lost my individual awareness to look where I pleased. I was now joined in what seemed to be a universal oneness in song. I was one with all the Heavens. I was one with more than the angels, the people, etc. I was ONE WITH what I knew to be the animals, the water, the sky, the stars, the plants, the trees, and the whole creation. I was joined into this spontaneous song that we all instantly began singing at the same time!

I cried out Holy. Oh, I cried out, "HOLY!!!! HOLY! HOOOOOOOLY, HOLY, HOLY!" Oh, I moved my arms!

I sang Holy and lost it. I have no idea how long I was there. I lost individuality. I was caught up. I just know that I was one with everyone. I was there for an unknown amount of time. I was in the most pleasurable experience of my created existence.

I came to for a bit. The Father began to sing thunderous affirmations to us. It was God's language. I don't have the ability to repeat. He was singing. He thundered. I was so lost in the moment that I wasn't afraid, not trembling, not crying. Just frozen in some holy stone like God moment. The father's ripple of words coming from the throne smacked me hard. I took it in like a microwave cooking popcorn. How do I explain this? I felt like I was being cooked and I was popping out and becoming larger and filling up. I was taking in the waves of His love, His goodness, His acceptance, His Peace. He was singing or was He thundering over His creation? He was pushing back a part of Himself into me and it was obvious into all of those within the kingdom. I was just enamored.

Heaven Awaits Your Expression

I was in a holy pause. I was swelling up inside with newly transformed particles of God within me. I felt like I was given new precious discoveries of God.

It seemed to build me into more of Him. Oh, this is hard to explain. I was taking Him into me and all of me was zapped up into Him. I was the sacrifice that was sucked right up until there was nothing left of me to give and then God just exploded into a push back of Himself into all the creation. All the creation seemed like they were running in a desert towards an oasis of water. It seemed the whole creation was desperate and dying of thirst. The father just let us drink to our soul's content. We dived in…drank from inside the water. How do you explain that?

On Earth I've never jumped into the ocean and drank water from underneath the water. Is that even possible? I guess it is. But I've never done it. Never. But here I felt like I was completely submerged in water, in light, and drinking it in! Oh, I was soaking up all of God I could! I just soaked. I wept more. I was so happy.

I was so excited to know Him and to experience Him. I was so completely aware of Him. Time just seemed to last. I know it is eternity there, but from our understanding, I was lost in my awareness of time.

It rained in Heaven. It was light. It rained everywhere. Light was everywhere already. But try to imagine brighter beams of light just raining everywhere. All creation was soaking it up. All of creation was waking up into a new dawn of a day. It was just as the sun was rising on the Earth. The old light of Heaven was being swallowed by new light. Oh, this is amazing. How could this be? It was as the brightness his creation experienced was turning brighter. All of Heaven brightened, reflected this light, took it in, and gave it out. Everyone and everything were being filled with light, absorbing it like energy, and begin to reflect the light outward more.

I turned to see some trees on the edges of the street. One such tree was taking the light in and blossoming all its created expressive fruit, flowers, and leaves back to the Father in its fullest of beauty.

Heaven Awaits Your Expression

The tree gave off new color, new light from its expression, and gave off a new holy glory. I realized something then.

I realized that all of God's creation just went from one glory to another glory.

Every encounter with the Father never left them the same. Each encounter took them from a past moment's glory…into a new moment's glory. Each created being was giving off a more glorious brighter expressive glory! Oh, the joys! Oh, the wonder! They were being transformed by the Father's nature to be more glorious in their expressive image bearing that they were designed to give out. They were now expressing another degree of The Father's image to all the other host of Heaven that would now have the blessing to experience once they interact with each other. This was beyond any human experience! Or was it? I was here for a reason.

I was here to learn how Heaven is, in order to bring Heaven to Earth. Earth is to be like Heaven where the sons of God are. We are a colony of Heaven on Earth. We are supposed to bring those lost on Earth into a demonstration of Heaven on Earth. We are to preach the kingdom of God. Teach Heaven's realties to the world. That's what Jesus did. He demonstrated God on Earth. He healed, delivered, saved, forgave, He gave joy, He gave wisdom from Heaven, He multiplied bread and fish, He walked on water, He calmed storms, He raised the dead.

He told Peter to catch a fish and take the gold coin out of the fish's mouth to pay their taxes. He told the disciples to cast their net on the other side and they caught enough fish to sink two boats. He said, "I am he" to the temple soldiers in the garden when they came to arrest him, and all the soldiers fell back on the ground as dead. He cast out many demons and did many other miracles all of which demonstrated the kingdom of Heaven. The kingdom of God. Jesus told the Pharisees that when He casts out a demon, the Kingdom of God has come upon them!

Jesus touched me. He said, "Brock, let's continue. You have experienced the worship of Heaven. You have experienced what I have explained to you. Did you see and feel how connected you are to all those within My Creation?

Heaven Awaits Your Expression

I know you did. I am in you and you are in Me. The Spirit that's within you is fully within Me. When Heaven joins in assembled worship, it's not just us worshipping here. It is all of my righteous ones.

You see, when the Spirit is following my command to worship, He calls all of my creation into worship. All of those on Earth hearing the call joins in. Those you saw in the sky, those down the street are spirits of just men and women who have obtained their prepared places here in Heaven. You may talk to any you please."

Jesus continued, "At the throne room, you will see the worship of those joining from Earth. They get to come boldly to the Throne of Grace anytime they please. That's where the Spirit's manifested light, torches, and constant access points are for believers. The throne is made of the temple of Heaven, the sea of glass/crystal that you read about in the Bible, and of the elder's thrones, my throne, and many cherubs, seraphim, and angels alike. All of Heaven can go worship at the throne at any time. They can worship from their homes, from the sky, the water, the forests, etc. Anywhere they please, they can join in worship. Those on Earth can enter the throne's place of worship anytime. By the Spirit, they have access to worship as in person."

Jesus continued, "If my people would understand that the Spirit in them is the same as the Spirit in My Father, and in Me...they would know that as soon as they yield and enter fully into my Spirit- they are present before the Father. They are one with me. One with the Spirit. They are one with the Father. The Spirit is the window into throne room realities on Earth. The Spirit's pleasure is to glorify our Heavenly realities to those called by our name on the Earth. We desire greatly to manifest ourselves to those who worship and call upon our name. Our presence, our light, our glory, is so honorable, so pure, and so holy that the measures at which people can experience depend upon the hearts of those praising. We will not allow our presence to be tread upon lightly. The blood of Jesus covers believers and the Spirit hides them from any judgment. They are recreated sons. But sons who disrespect the presence of their God are still babies, toddlers, etc. The sons need raising. They cannot yield to sin. They cannot join and partner with sin.

Heaven Awaits Your Expression

It will cause them to fall away! The sons of God need training, discipling, and weaning off the milk. They will experience a lot of My presence and power as newborns, toddlers, etc....but training in righteousness continues on towards greater responsibility, influence, and placement. Sons who choose obedience whole heartedly are going forward to greater responsible training. You have my Spirit already. You have all the power of the universe at your disposal and you have authority to use it because of your position as a Son of God."

Jesus pressed on, "You are not trained to responsibly operate the power until I deem so. You receive power once you are baptized with my Spirit. I have given all those with my Spirit the authority and power to heal all diseases and cast out demons. But the skill to demonstrate openly my kingdom as Jesus did comes only through testing, training, and dying to self. You must be trained as a son. You must be disciplined into the Son of God responsibilities. Brock, learning those responsibilities, practicing them with me, and going through the necessary training is what is required. You possess ALL power already. I must help you know me, know your placement, and teach you to walk in my instruction as I desire you to. Growing in this training and continue growing in the grace of whom you were designed to be is the process we begin now."

Jesus noted, "This is how you learn of me and my ways. You will have many opportunities to practice in between our sessions. As you come before Me, I'll answer all questions, teach you all things, guide you into all truth, and demonstrate accordingly all that you need to know. You will need to be patient, be persistent, and be diligent to steward this responsibility well. You have my Spirit and all things are possible because of Him. You can do anything by the Spirit. Not one thing done on the Earth is capable of accomplishment WITHOUT HIM."

"Brock, Let's walk." He said. I followed in a holy hush. I followed and watched him step on each golden brick. I watched every brick knowing now that each of them praised and vibrated knowing that Jesus walked over them. They were alive! What a revelation!

We stopped. We were on this gold bricked road. What was the name of this road? I looked and there was a road sign. It said,
"The Way of Righteousness".

Heaven Awaits Your Expression

CHAPTER 10

JAMI'S MANSION

"The architecture, design, plant life, and everything else in her home is an ocean front atmosphere for eternity."

I looked around. There were buildings. Each building had a different stone architecture. One had terra cotta looking roof tiles on top. Others had flat smooth golden slopes on the roof. It was as if the roofs were completely artistically designed custom for each house. Yes, I sold roofs, so instinctively I was looking at the roofs first. I was seeing no repair work needed! I saw many different kinds of roofs! Some houses/buildings didn't even seem to have a roof. I wondered if they needed one here.

The stone on the walls was a yellow orange marble. I've never seen houses built with marble like this. It was like the whole house I was looking at was on a corner. It was made of a golden like marble. It looked like the whole house was carved out of one stone! I've seen large countertops carved out, but this whole 3 story house was one exterior piece of golden marble like stone structure! It was absolutely stunning! The windows didn't have windows! There was no glass. If there was, I couldn't see it. It was carved with epic designs.

Heaven Awaits Your Expression

It was most certainly the work of an artist. The exterior stone wall had the design of waves of an ocean rippling from all around a window flowing towards the window. It was like the window was the beach head. The waves looked exactly like what you see in an aerial photo of an island. The waves were rippling in and turning into concave like waves as they came in closer to the window.

Somehow my vision was zooming in. It seemed like it was so real looking. I think I saw the waves moving! I feel like the golden marble was made to have a live action ocean front feel. I think I can see the waves moving gently into the window! How in the world did they do that?

I heard Jesus inside me telling me that it's like the gold brick. The atoms are responsive to the desires of the person who lives there. She really loved the ocean front. Her home was created to give off the feel of ocean front. The architecture, design, plant life, and everything else in her home is an ocean front atmosphere for eternity. Wow! So, it was moving! That is amazing! I've never seen that in my Earth life!

I looked and there was a woman looking out of the window at me. Well, actually, she was looking at Jesus with tears in her eyes. Jesus was conversing with her silently. She cried and smiled. They looked, talked from within, and she nodded in humble respect, and turned to look at me. She then gave a knowing smile telling me that she knew she gets to talk to me. She left behind the window and walked down. I didn't see her and then I did. She came right up to me. She knew I wasn't a residing homesteader yet. I was still on Earth visiting in the Spirit.

She said, "Hello" and just stood there smiling. Radiating. Just a beautiful smile. I took her to be of Pilipino descent. I think.

I shyly said, "Hello!"

She said, "You like my house?

I was off my game. I'm usually very people oriented and love to carry on a conversation with perfect strangers.

I have found that to be one of my proudest character traits. I love talking to people!

Heaven Awaits Your Expression

I love having nice pleasant conversations and connect with people. I love connecting and making perfect strangers smile!

But now I'm standing here in Heaven, being greeted by my first person other than Jesus and the angels! She simply walked up and said, "Hello" to me. I was slow to respond. I mean, not only was she standing and smiling at me, but Jesus was standing there. Have you ever had a conversation with Jesus standing there???

Um no. I never have.

I mean, now I realize that He is standing with me by the Spirit in every conversation. I know He is there in every conversation…at all times…in all things. Everything I do, I am in union with Him and He is with me. Standing in Me, as if a window from His Person to mine, Jesus is a part of everything we do through the Spirit. I know all that! But I've never stood and talked with anyone with Jesus standing there beside me. I was shocked a bit by how I could be nervous in Heaven. But it wasn't really a nervousness. It was more of a new experience; it was my first time. There were firsts in Heaven- an eternity of first times! Once you are brought into your first time, you renew into a more experienced being. I was such a baby at this!

I looked back at the lady. This is pretty wild. I saw this beautiful tanned faced lady seemingly in her thirties standing before me. I could also see a glimpse of her in her past human years. Back then, I saw her as tired, hard worked, sun baked, and the color pigmentation differences in the skin on her face from the scarcity of nutrition, I guess. I saw her living on an island. She had a humble home on the ocean. Seaside. She lost her life on Earth from a tsunami. She was swept away by water and hit on the head with debris and drowned horribly into blackness as she lost consciousness in the muddy waters.

She died in water and appeared with the angels at the veil of Heaven. She was a born-again believer on the Earth. I knew this much just by looking at her. How? I think in Heaven everyone has knowledge about one another.

I felt Jesus encourage me to have a conversation with this woman.

I smiled back at the pretty lady. I said, "And Hello to you as well".

Heaven Awaits Your Expression

I mustered up my best southern charm and said it in the most pleasant expressions that I could give with all the kindness I could muster. I was talking in front of Jesus!

I felt Jesus moving on my insides. He was speaking to my inner man. He was intuitively reminding me that He was within me. No need to think about Jesus standing there. I was in Him and He was in me! The Spirit was the same in both of us. He somehow supernaturally brought understanding to me that each time I talk with others, I just have to yield to the Spirit of our Father to speak within me. He said to me, "Brock, every time you speak to a person, it's as WE are speaking. You must use every word in a yielding and co-working unison with the Spirit. Brock, every interaction you have with others, you do with my Spirit and I involved. You must understand that every interaction you have is ordained and orchestrated by Heaven. I have asked this woman to speak with you. Now, let's practice. Talk in your yielded place in Me. Let every word be drenched with the Grace and Life of the Spirit. Yes, even your common talk can carry my unction. Brock, words are things. They are created vibrations and light. I'll tell you more about your words later. Keep talking."

"I LOVE your home! It's absolutely gorgeous and it stopped me in my tracks and has me in wonder! I can feel the ocean front, the seaside, and the island feel. I see you are from the islands?" I said smoothly and freely from all my own trying. I was yielded and the words came to me without any striving.

I just let the words flow from my mouth, move out from my eyes, and my body moved in unison. They all seemed to be in genuine fluid movements as I joined in a conversation with this lady. It was really special.

By yielding to the Lord in communications with this lady, I was in essence given permission by her. I was giving permission to her from me as well. We gave an inward permission to one another to connect. I could instantly know her. She was then knowing me. There was a loving family awareness of one another. We knew one another. We were long time family and close. We were of the same tribe.

Heaven Awaits Your Expression

This was new. How in the world was I connected to this lady in just my first interaction?

Jesus spoke within and reminded me that, "He that is in Christ is neither Jew nor Greek. There's no difference in American or Pilipino. It's not male nor female. It is Christ. He is All in All."

The Same Spirit in Christ was in her and in me. By the Spirit, I knew her and her likewise with me. This was different to me.

She smiled and confirmed, "Yes, I was from the islands. I lived humbly on the side of the sea. I had few family and few loved ones. A missionary there led me to Jesus. I lived with the sound of the waves crashing against large rocks. I have loved that sound my whole life. Now, I get to enjoy it for all of eternity! I was given this home by Jesus when I arrived. He loves each of us so individually. He treats us as His very own. We are His family! I didn't have much family on Earth. Nor did I have a lot of people around. I was lonely. Here, I get to live in this city and enjoy being around people for eternity AND I get to hear the ocean sound and see the waves in my home! I am blessed as a daughter of the King. I am eternally grateful and I'm proud I get to share with you!"

This was a special moment. I thought to myself, "I wonder what it's like inside her home?" And right then, I heard back, "Sure, please! Be my guest…please follow me!" She was talking to me inside like Jesus did! So, I can talk to people here inside and out? Wow!

Then, I wondered and thought I might as well ask inside to test this out, "So, you can talk with me inside my mind?"

She gave a little giggle and said, "Yes. We can talk inside to one another once each have given permission. We are so respectful to one another here. Each of us see the individual greatness in one another and honor one another. Everyone is extremely loving, thoughtful, and very giving! People love more than anything to serve one another and give to one another."

She kept walking and I followed. Jesus offered to let me walk with her ahead of him. I thought that was really amazing that the King of the Universe would offer such kind gestures to a guy like me!

Heaven Awaits Your Expression

What was that? In my world, if the President of the United States came into a room, I would get pushed aside by his Secret Service bodyguards and I would most certainly be giving way for him to walk into a room first. It's the honorable and respectable thing to do. But here...with Jesus, He just let me walk first! Whew! I was about to cry.

The lady could feel and hear me thinking. She said, "See, I told you! Jesus is the most honorable and respectful of all! He shows the most breathtakingly respect to all His creation. His people give honor to Jesus for all of eternity! No one ever misses a moment to see Jesus! Everyone loves Jesus and lives to please Him here!"

I followed along. I was starting to open my mind. I knew that once I began to think, I would have a million questions. Then it hit me. I wondered what was this lady's name? Then it came up in my intuition, "Jamiba, is your name! Jamiba, nice to meet you. I knew your name? Wow this is amazing. I know anyone's name I meet?"

She said, "Yes, Brock, I know yours as well. When you greet another person here, you show kindness, accept one another, you know other's names, and then you will each give permission inside for one another to "know" each other.

Once you do, the other person will know you by more than your name and have access to know more about you by the Spirit. We are so connected here! The Spirit is fully alive in everyone and we all love others as the Lord has loved us!"

She stopped and turned to me and put her hands together in a prayer stance and slightly bowed respectively. I knew this must've been a custom to her where she was from. It was very polite, and I was finding myself doing the same back to her in response. I bowed, smiled, and politely followed her gesture to come up the few steps into her home.

The steps were golden sand. It looked like it was a sand dollar carved out of sands right on the beach- but made in gold. It was golden sand!

Heaven Awaits Your Expression

Wow. She knew my thoughts and she said she was thrilled the first time she saw the steps. She said it was one of the first experiences in Heaven that is still a wonder to this day.

She said she has had that wonder and amazement about her steps since day one and it's stuck with her now for the whole time.

I wanted to ask, "How long have you been in Heaven?" She responded to me in a funny way, "Well, since the day I died on Earth." She smiled and wondered. She looked at Jesus. Jesus said to both of us inside, "She perished 325 years ago on Earth. She has been in this home since the moment I introduced it to her."

~

After I was free to research. I looked up the weather data we have on record online. I found what may be the storm this lady passed away during.

325 years ago, was 1694. We have historical data that there was a major storm that killed over 400 people in the Philippines area: https://en.wikipedia.org/wiki/List_of_Pacific_typhoons_before_1850

~

"Ok, that is just amazing. Thank you for letting me come into your home." I smiled and I genuinely felt so honored that she would let me come into her mansion.

Oh, it was nice! The steps were made of golden sand! The handrails were made of what looked like sand dollar. It was a sand dollar material that was carved eloquently to be a work of art! The door was breathtaking! The door wasn't a door like what we have. It did not have hinges. It was not a door. It was a doorway only. The only thing that separated out the threshold was beautiful streams of water! The water came straight down in a straight flow down into almost a wall of water. It didn't separate until about halfway down. The water seemed to be a pure flow of water like a perfectly flowing waterfall that had no disturbance in the flow. It was beautiful!

Heaven Awaits Your Expression

She watched me closely to see what I would do. I waited and she said to me within, "Just walk right through the water" and well, that's exactly what I did! I stepped across the little porch area, and I was pleased to feel the golden sand on my feet! The sand actually felt like I was walking on sand at the beach!

I just smiled, took it in, and kept walking into the waterfall doorway. When I stepped into the threshold, the water hit my body like a gentle massage! It came over me like a smooth gentle ice cream. I didn't get wet at all. It just flowed over me and went right into the bottom drain at the bottom of the threshold.

I stepped in and turned around in silent wonder. I watched Jesus step through. He stepped into this woman's home and I felt His presence as He was sending His peace into the room. He was doing what He said for His disciples to do in Luke 10! He gave the home His peace! The house responded with the resounding hum and vibration of an instrument as you begin warming up. It was coming alive.

I looked around and I couldn't believe what I saw! She had alive trees inside her home! She had a waterfall coming from her third story section of the home!

Vines went up the walls, flowers were blossoming and bursting out at the presence of Jesus! Jesus was turning the place into a gorgeous wonderland! There were birds letting off the branches and flapping their wings rapidly in praise as they descended from the trees. They were coming down to the floor of the home to be on the ground and they began to spread their wings out wide. One looked like a parrot or some kind of tropical bird. I realized that possibly this was what on Earth she enjoyed the most!

Again, she knew my thoughts. Somehow, she walked up beside me and I didn't even feel her walk up to me. She begins to look at Jesus and I and say, "Welcome into my home. We honor the name of Jesus and honor your presence Lord! We give you all the glory and the honor and all the praise! You have delivered me from my witchcraft and fornication and sent your servant to my island to speak to me the words of life and I was born again as your child! I was a nobody. I was lonely and without a father…and you became a father to me! I was orphaned and you fathered me! I was without love and you loved me! I was hungry and you fed me! I was thirsty and you gave me drink!

You are worthy! You are mighty! You are the King of Glory!"

She kept on! I found myself on the floor face down and singing word for word with her this spontaneous song she was singing to the Lord! I felt the hum of the gold under my whole body! I sang and the gold made ripples where my mouth was!

I noticed something entirely different than on Earth! I was singing and worshipping on my face to the Lord on a golden floor and there was no snot! I was baffled! I was momentarily distracted with a split-second thought! I said, "There is no snot! I'm not snotting here in Heaven!" And then I began to worship and praise the Lord for no snot! I was so overwhelmed by the revelation of no snot! Yes. Seriously! There was no snot! That's the worst thing about being on your face before the Lord on the Earth is all the snot that comes out and drips all over your floor! My carpet has been smeared many times! Here I could give Him all the praise I wanted and not have to deal with that!

She began to slow down and I followed. Jesus began to push back a glorious energy that strengthened us to go on. We felt honored and He did as well. I don't know how to explain it, but she was honored for Jesus to be in her home. She was honored that I came to her home. Jesus was honored to be there and welcomed. Jesus was honored that I was there! I was honored to even be there in Heaven at all! Let alone be with Jesus! Beautifully enough, I was honored and fully grateful to be in this lady's home.

She began to tell me how she loved these tropical birds on Earth! These birds gave her company when she was lonely. She told me how that when she was lonely, she would pray to the Lord and He would send these birds to fly onto the branches on the trees by her home. She would talk to the birds and they would listen to her. They would talk back and make noises.

Heaven Awaits Your Expression

They truly did respond and seemed to talk to her. Now, in Heaven she can truly talk to the birds! She can inwardly talk to the birds and they talk back!

I asked if she could show me! She asked the bird beside her to fly up and land on my arm. Sure enough, the bird did a courtesy bow to her and to Jesus, flapped its wings a couple of times and was peacefully landing on my arm. The bird's eye was looking into mine and willing for me to allow him to interact with me.

I said, "Hello little friend, please, by all means, you are welcome to know me as well!"

Then I heard the bird speak to me! He said, "Hello Brock! I have waited to speak with you! Once you were outside, we could feel the presence of Jesus!
We knew that if you were with Jesus then we wanted to know you!"

I was just amazed at this bird. This bird seemed so wise! This bird seemed so confident, sure of himself, and eloquent in his speech. I was like inwardly trying to make sense of this! The only other animals that spoke to me was the lion and the deer. The lion was king-like in his talking to me and now this bird was extremely smart and savvy. I looked back at the bird and smiled with not much to say...I just said the first thing that came to my mind, "What is your name?"

He said, "I am Jalal, I go by Jala... I am at your service"

Wow. I responded, "Ok, Jala, I am Brock Knight. I am from the USA and I have many birds that live and feed from my property. I love birds! I haven't until now ever heard a bird speak to me! You are my very first. I'm honored to have spoken to you for the first of all birds! May I ask if you were on the Earth? Did you die and come here?"

He shook his head saying, "No, I was never on your Earth. I have lived here from eternity long. I was created to give my praises to the Lord and to bless His name with the other birds. I found pleasure in speaking and living here with Jami. She finds pleasure in talking with me and I find completeness in meeting her needs!

Heaven Awaits Your Expression

I have been invited to serve here with her since the day before she arrived. Jesus prepared me for her coming and I was ready. I welcomed her as I welcomed you. It was the most beautiful of unions.

Jala, the tropical bird, gave me a courtesy bow again and lifted off and landed back in his posture of praise and honor before the Lord of Hosts and us. I just took in this bird. I just spoke to a bird! I looked at him bowing to the Lord. It reminded me of the Lion King movie when they would bow to the King Mufasa and Simba.

This Jala was a beautiful bird. He was at least five feet wide when he opened his wings. He was blue and gold. He had some white in there and some color close to a yellow.

It was a beautiful design. It was the kind of color that you would expect to be in a very expensive jewelry store. He would be a very famous bird on the Earth!

Jamiba, who I found out goes by Jami as well, stood and began to describe the significance of the waterfall, the sound of the ocean coming from her back balcony. She showed me beautiful art on her wall, surrounded by plant life growing perfectly around the frame. The frame was made of perfectly carved driftwood. It was so pretty.

She had a transparent roof! The roof was see-through. She said that she lays in her hammock some days and just worships the Lord as the colors from The Father's presence roll across the sky! She loves to star gaze and listen for certain activity around the city.

She said that she can hear kids playing, worship, music being created, and announcements being made. She leaves her beautiful sanctuary home and goes down the street and talks to people all day! She goes to certain folks who carve her precious items as gifts, sing her songs, dance for her, read books to her, recite poetry to her, paint for her, preach the wonders of God to her, and sometimes she goes to watch the happenings of the people on Earth. She can check on those from her island to see if the promises of God about revival and salvation are coming to pass on her islands.

Heaven Awaits Your Expression

She then said that she had one special thing to show me. She brought me to a separate room, and it was a workshop. She said, "Brock, my passion in Heaven is to build special toys custom made for kids. I like to find kids here and bless them with a toy that I've made perfectly for them!

These toys can interact with them and sing songs to them!" She went and pulled out a toy GI Joe. This GI Joe didn't have guns. It had swords on the side. It was an Earthly soldier with Heavenly weapons! Oh, I started to realize what she was doing!

That was for me!

"That's for me?" I asked.

She nodded enthusiastically and said, "It would please you to have this toy?"

I started to have tears in my eyes, and said, "Yes, that toy is perfect for me! I loved GI Joes as a young boy! Thank you so much! That was the nicest gift! Thank you Jami!"

I found myself crying again. I was feeling this scripture inside about my tears. Yes, there are tears in Heaven! The Word says that he will wipe away your tears – meaning, you have tears. But they are not sad or depressed tears. Here there are only tears of joy and overwhelming peace.

> **Revelation 7:17 (KJV)**
> **For the Lamb which is in the midst of the throne shall feed them, and shall lead them unto living fountains of waters: and God shall <u>wipe away all tears from their eyes</u>.**

I felt so much emotion from this lady's generosity! The respect she showed. The honor. The precious acceptance, attention, hospitality, and connection I felt with this lady was just beautiful. I've known her but for a few moments and I'm so in sync with her. Oh, I felt so loved! She walked to me and gave the same courtesy bow and presented me with the gift. I was crying in such a peaceful way.

Heaven Awaits Your Expression

Then, I realized that I had no gift to give her! I felt sad…or I started to. She looked at Jesus. Jesus spoke to us and warmed our hearts. He said to both of us out loud, "Children, this is bringing me great joy to see that you love one another. By this, I know my followers are my disciples indeed.

Brock, your presence here is a gift to her, and by honoring her by telling the whole world. By telling her story to the whole world, you will give the gift of greatest honor. Making her name a memorial in time is greatly honored to a citizen of Heaven. Tell my people of how I honor the least of these my people. Tell them how I love even those who are lonely and stranded. Tell them that in Heaven, even those who on Earth are forgotten and lowly, I prepare a mansion for. I visit them, love them, and give all of my delights to for all eternity!

Tell them to love as I love, honor as I honor, give as I give, and serve as I serve! Tell them to not treat any person as common or unworthy. All people are fearfully and wonderfully made! All of My creation, every last atom, the rocks, soil, water, air, trees, plants, and animals are all treated with honor and respect! Tell them to give more than they receive! Tell them to honor God and honor all people! Make sure they hear that in Heaven, the most treaded upon brick of gold, the most unknown orphaned lady from the islands, and a bird created for Heaven's beauty are all loved by Jesus and each enjoy giving their designed expression to Me in worship! I love and honor them all! I am their God and they are mine! We are connected and live and breathe as one! All are welcome and All are loved!"

Oh, I cried even more! Jesus was so great! He is so wonderful and awesome and glorious! I wanted to praise Him for eternity long! I was so full of peace, joy, love, and light! I know I was radiating like a star with His light! I felt like I was glowing from His presence and radiance! I felt like the moon. I was reflecting His light off every part of my body!

Jesus thanked the birds and Jami. He bowed His head in respect and told us all that we must be moving on. Jami and Jala and all the other birds all bowed back. Just this act of saying bye was precious and wonderful to behold. I mean, who wants Jesus to leave you?

Heaven Awaits Your Expression

Who wants Him to be so close and then leave? Oh, I just raised my eyebrows like, "Ok everyone, I'm with Him! I'll see you all again someday! Love you all and grace and peace be unto you all! Be blessed and eternally fulfilled!"

I walked out with Jesus and we were instantly back on the road. Jesus looked at me. He looked INTO me. He seemed to be reading into me to see if I was fully grasping His training. He said, "Brock, you are seeing how I honor people. I honor all of My creation. Honor is due to all who have been created to give expression of their Maker. Give Honor to whom Honor is due. To those I've placed in authority to help and guide you, give honor. Do what is right. Follow your conscience, your wisdom, your counsel, and make the right decisions.

Acknowledge Me with each decision and I'll always direct your path correctly. To live in honor is to live with My character, My nature, and My integrity. My Spirit is in you and you possess all the power and ability to make right decisions all the days of your life! You can live as I designed you to live! Just yield to Me and allow Me to live in you and through you!"

"Brock, how did it feel to receive the love, respect, and gift from Jami?" Jesus asked me.

I responded, "It was amazing. It moved me to tears. I felt so moved and touched. I think I should use that same heart of love and honor on Earth. Right?"

"Yes, please. You must love and lead my people. I want you to be an example of love and honor. I want you to have this same effect on others on Earth as you experienced it here in Heaven. If you yield and submit yourself to the Spirit within you, then you will grow in your ability to love others this way. I'll begin to produce many ways for you to give to others. I'll give you neat ways to give gifts. Try to accumulate many gifts to give and have them with you. Send them in the mail. Email them. Have your gifts special delivered to the people's front doors. Make giving such a big deal! Give in a way that exposes Heaven to the person! I want people to experience My presence as they receive your gift!

Heaven Awaits Your Expression

You will learn as I give opportunity to you. You will know what to do! I want my sons to be THE EXAMPLES in giving! I want my family to be known for radiant giving! Extremely cheerful and exciting giving! I want to see my Spirit freeing, healing, and delivering simply from the result of a generous gift! You will see more of this as you grow!"

"Yes Lord, I will be that son for you! I will give! I will give with all my soul! I will bring Heaven to Earth in giving with outrageous generosity and give glory to your name! Oh Lord, thank you thank you thank you! Thank you for showing me how powerful and amazing the love and generosity of your people is here! Oh, I hope to become a champion on the Earth in giving! Oh Lord! I pray you allow me to inspire your people to give with a Heavenly purpose! Oh Lord!

Teach me more about giving! I want to know how to give with the love, attention, and ability as you give!"

Heaven Awaits Your Expression

CHAPTER 11

JESUS GLORIFIED

"The Earth, the stone, the gold I walked on, and even the walls seem to become alive with the familiar hum.

Jesus lifted His hands and we disappeared. We instantly appeared somewhere else. We were standing at what looked like a library! I looked to my left and there were miles and miles of columns and pillars of the most beautiful ivory granite like stonework carved by the most skillful angels. I was imagining that only angels could've accomplished this. These pillars looked to be made of one single stone. There were no cracks, not individual stones, or anything that would show they were in any separate pieces. It looked like miles and miles of ONE SOLID PIECE OF STONE!

There were open walls with just pillars every 30-40 feet. I was experiencing beautiful light outside, the sound of birds, beautiful worship filled atmosphere, and a hum of perfect atmospheric beauty all around. It was as if the atmosphere was charged with an expectancy at all times of the glory clouds of God crashing down upon us.

I felt like all of the angels around, rocks, plants, birds, animals, sky, stars, ground, pillars of stone, and all of the massive amount of books before me were all alive and instantly ready to go into a chorus of ecstatic worship together.

Then I reminded myself, that I'm walking through Heaven with JESUS and that's probably why everywhere I go is completely charged with the atom bomb like intensity. I must be experiencing what it's like when all of creation knows He is near. It seems a fusion of all life forms begins to react to His presence. It seems all the atoms begin to be charged, to move actively, causing friction from all the energetic movement to be felt within every atom of my own body.

Just then I pictured every single atom within eyesight around the person of Jesus being charged to an extreme electric excitement. I see the air I'm breathing being charged with a thick mass of atoms. The air itself becomes thicker than it was before Jesus came. It's like the air around Jesus becomes denser. Could it be that atoms from miles away rush to the presence of Jesus to be alive and fully renewed just like the people do? The Earth, the stone, the gold I walked on, and even the walls seem to become alive with the familiar hum. It's becoming clearer now! The atoms within the stone are moving at the expectancy of their Creator nearby! The stone is alive! The ground moves with an unreal life of its own that I've never experienced. Jesus is here! All of creation declares His Glory! All beings alike praise Him! How wonderful!

It reminded me of the scripture:

Luke 19:40
> **40 And he answered and said unto them, I tell you that, if these (little children) should hold their peace, <u>the stones would immediately cry out.</u>**

Jesus looked around, smiled, and gave a glorious wave of His hand and all of creation came under a holy hush, a silent wonder, and right then I felt like all eyes were on us. I sensed with my knowing intuition that angels were in the sky above us watching. I thought of it and instantly Jesus was inside me giving me permission.

Heaven Awaits Your Expression

I looked up and oh, I bent my knees in a startled terror at first. I realized I was in Heaven and this is a normal thing, right? But when I saw the many angels standing in the sky,

I almost didn't have my natural mind's ability to process it. I looked up and angels in pure white clothing were standing in the air! It looked like they were standing on something, but that something was thin air. They were looking at me and Jesus! They were looking like what Greek gods look like. They were like living statues of glorious bodies! They seemed to be reflecting the Father's light directly at the right angle…right into my eyes! I held my hand up to block the blinding light, but they were so bright!

Jesus was willing me to look back at Him. I turned.

~

I was turning myself toward the Lord. Something was different. This all happened in the twinkling of an eye. I'm going to do my best to describe what was bombarding my whole being in such a nanosecond of time. It was as if I was in the Airforce and tasked to observe the Atomic Bomb testing up close and personal. Just imagine being up close to an atomic bomb explosion. Just picture the moment when the instant change of the whole atmosphere turns to the most blinding white light you've ever experienced.

The Earth shakes, sound is deactivated in your senses. The whole planet is changed instantly into another environment! Just imagine everything within you being pulled apart and all within the slightest of a thought.

I was completely swallowed by light! I thought the light from the angels were fearful and unbearable! I had thought the light they were blinding me with came from the Father! But I was wrong! Oh, I was terribly wrong! It was ALL JESUS! He was now shining in all His Glory! Oh, He was not shining per se. He was. He simply WAS. HE WAS BEING. He was not holding it back! Glory and Power and Life and Light and Virtue and All of His nature was emanating out of Him and it was TERRIFYING!

He was now pure lightning in front of me. I grew stiff and frozen. I was completely frozen. Now the angels and Jesus were both shining, and the light was literally going through my being... right through me! It was passing through from all directions!

How do I explain that? The light was terribly messing up the organization of my whole being. I could sense that there were particles of ME everywhere. Who knows where every bit of me was? Oh, this is hard to describe. I am trying to describe the nano-parts of a second in time. But there's no time there, so this moment simply STARTED. I have no clue how long it occurred.

The whole building was lost in the light. I was in complete nothingness...just absolutely nothing but the flash. Ugh, how do I explain. It's not light as we know it! It's like taking the instance of a lightning flash and multiply it by some huge number, then keep that flash, that brightness, and make the overwhelming flash last a long time. Imagine being stuck in that flash without protective goggles! Imagine closing your eyes and you keep willing yourself to close your eyes, and no matter what...your eyes being closed doesn't change the brightness! The eyelids don't affect the brightness! You are swallowed up in brightness. I was being blinded it seemed even down in my organs.

My insides were feeling the brightness! The light was touching every part of me! The light was seeming to pass straight through me.

I lost orientation. I completely lost what was up and down, left or right, or in front or behind me. I don't know how to properly explain that either. I just know that in the pure light flash of the lightning countenance of Jesus I couldn't find my orientation at all. It was overwhelmingly beyond me and I was completely in a nothingness...but Jesus. I was on the ground. I was willing to be dead on my face, completely surrendered. Nothing I willed occurred. I was just frozen and at the mercy of God. I gave in to dying. I gave in to the force of energy pulling all of me in. I realized then that Jesus was GOD. HE WAS THE I AM. He was as much God as the Father! He was the absolute express image of the Father! He is so loving and approachable and all by HIS MERCY!

The scripture was in my soul, "Be still and know that I am God".

Heaven Awaits Your Expression

The stillness went on for so long. In the stillness, I completely changed everything I knew about Jesus. I saw Him as God Almighty.

I saw Him as the Great and Terrible, the Great Love, the Great Mercy, The Great Judge, The Great I AM, He was Great. He was to be Feared, Reverenced, Respected, Honored. Jesus was to be worshipped! He was to be glorified! He was the Creator of All Things. He was an all-consuming fire too! Jesus became a man in order to free us…God became a little ole man to adopt us and MAKE US LIKE HIM. Oh, everything about Jesus in my heart, soul, & mind changed.

Oh, I was in the light and I was born again. I was baptized in light. I found something there that I've never gathered on Earth. That's all I can say about that. I pray every person experiences the removal of all darkness and shadows from your spirit, soul, and body. I pray you experience light permeate every part of your organs, your brain, your toes, and all that's in between. I pray you feel what it's like to be blinded and not know if you are alive or dead, up or down, here or there, just a lightning flash through your being that lasts for 10,000 moments! One day you will stand before Him as the Son of Man who is glorified as the Son of God. You will see him as the Judean/Jewish Hebrew man Jesus Christ from Nazareth on some occasions and then the opportunities will come to see Him High & Lifted Up and Glorified above all names! He is truly far above all principality, power, might, & dominions, and every name that is named, not only in this world, but also that which is to come! He is Jesus Christ, and He alone is preeminent. He is first. Everything that was created was created through Him. He is the fullness of the Godhead embodied. He's the express image of the Father of spirits - our Jehovah God! Jesus is truly the Alpha and the Omega, the first and the last. He alone holds the keys to life and death. All power in Heaven and in Earth is within his mouth. There is none like Him. Every knee will bow, and every tongue will confess that He is LORD.

Oh, the moments you have with Jesus! Oh, I pray you encounter Him and be born again over and over!

Jesus came into my view.

Heaven Awaits Your Expression

I was coming to.

I was together. Oh, the relief, the pleasure. The awareness that I obtained! I was seeing again!

The light was settling like dew to the grass. It was as if fog was in the air. It looked like the fog when you're driving, and you can't see past your windshield. It was thick. The fog was nothing more than light. Nothing but little particles of light. Was it particles? Wait, maybe all of those atoms in the air are experiencing what I'm experiencing? Maybe they too are filled with His majestic light and presence! Oh that's it!

It was like the Spirit inside of me put His finger on that thought. I knew He wanted me to discuss this topic with you who are reading this book. If you've made it this far in the book, then I guess you are hungry enough to hear the Lord on a very important matter to His people these days. The Body of Christ seems to be divided into a few camps when it comes to this topic.

The topic I'm referring to is about the EXTREMES that stem out of the Supernatural, the Glory of God, the Presence of God, the Miracles, The Healings, The Vision & Dreams, and the mystical uses of these Biblical experiences.

~

I would like to address this topic right now. It seems it was on the Heart of Jesus while I was there in Heaven. It's on His heart now. This has come to be one of the subjects I spend more time teaching on these days as I see more and more of the church asleep.

When I was experiencing the worship in Heaven and the Glory of Almighty God, I was clearly having some powerful experiences. The ability I had to take in the most minute details was beyond amazing. I could process many times over the amount my brain does here on Earth. I could see the many details of anything occurring. I have tried my best to relay these details in a way that allows the reader to experience it with me. At least, that's what I was trying to do. When I saw Jesus glorify Himself like this moment with Him by the library. I was even more illuminated or enlightened than at other times. It's pretty mind boggling how light can do that to you?

Heaven Awaits Your Expression

Light in your home exposes details around you. If a room was dark, you flip the switch and light comes on and the details that were hidden are now discoverable to the beholder.

Likewise, when the pure unspeakable light of Jesus was present, I could see even the smallest of atoms and particles around me! If you don't believe me, just wait till you go to Heaven. You tell me yourself how you would explain this.

Back to that moment. I knew then what the Bible referred to as "glory clouds" or when they say, "the glory of the Lord filled the temple, or "the glory cloud covered the mountain, etc." It was referring to exactly this.

What I was seeing up close with my powerful new Heavenly eyes was basically allowing me to see the science of Heavenly realities. When His presence is near, even the atoms and microbial life in the air are participating in the moment. They too get filled with the Spirit. They too are filled with light! They too experience it all! That explains how I've seen a thick atmosphere in certain worship experiences in church. You could look around and see the milky thick air filled with the substance of the Spirit of God. It's like a cloud can be perceived in the air sometimes after a time when two or three gathered have just experienced His amazing presence!

So many times, I've observed the faces of believers have a "glow" emanating from their faces after a worship experience (Like Moses when he came down from the mountain, or Stephen when he was being martyred). They seem to be extremely loving, have fullness of joy, and have peace that's clearly from God.

Some would say they have an aura about them, or a glow. New Agers would say they are giving off an energy, a zen, a chi, or a force. Who knows what terminology they've come up with now? I've heard many ways different groups explain the invisible tangible life of God that issues out of a person who's been with Jesus.

The woman with the issue of blood touched Jesus and there went virtue out of Him. The multitude of followers pressed in to touch Jesus and virtue went out from Him and healed them all.

Heaven Awaits Your Expression

In the Book of Acts, people came to Jerusalem and got close enough to have the shadow of Peter come across them and they were healed as well. How do you explain that?

The Apostle Paul was able to transmit this life and virtue into cloths or handkerchiefs and those cloths were laid on sick, diseased, demon possessed, and they were miraculously healed. They were delivered by coming into contact with the very life of God almighty on a cloth!

Some circles in the Body of Christ would call this the anointing. That's not an entirely accurate use of that term. The anointing is the LIFE, VIRTUE, & POWER of the Spirit of God that's present within all believers. The sons of God are THE ANOINTED. When the sons of God do what they are sent to do, the Spirit of the Lord does His work through them. That's the virtue, the life, the power of the Spirit at work. That's what people refer to as the anointing.

That life flows out from each believer. Out of their belly flows rivers of living water. That's life, virtue, & power flowing out of their inner man from the Spirit of God dwelling inside of them. When a believer is filled to overflowing with the Spirit, even the air around them is affected, the soil beneath them, animals present, and especially other humans! Every created being around them responds ON EARTH to the presence of their Creator just like in Heaven! It all makes more sense to me!

With my eyes in Heaven, I can see even the smallest of details! I wish I could take your mind right now as you read this book and make you see what I saw. I'm doing my best to cause the words that I choose here to paint a picture that does it justice.

I realized a clearer understanding of many scriptures throughout the Bible I've heard and studied. I heard folks talk about the presence of God all of my life. I've heard people talk about the Shekinah Glory of God, or the manifested Glory of God on the Earth. I myself have experienced the power of the Lord, the glory of the Lord, the glory cloud they refer to, and have experienced many displays of the anointing folks idolize throughout my life on Earth.

Heaven Awaits Your Expression

I have studied it thoroughly in the Bible and can teach on the subject seven ways to Sunday. I've also seen many extremes on this topic go to one extreme and also to the other extreme. The body of Christ is really derailed on this topic.

This topic of the presence of God, power, and mystical experiences has a biblical place throughout the whole Bible from Genesis all the way to Revelation. There is a solid biblically whole experience that stays close and holds tight to what the Bible says and keeps it in proper context. Everything about our experience with our God is supernatural. We are to live in the Spirit, be spiritual, and live practical normal lives in the natural. But too often, the people of God veer off in one direction or the other and we get into extremes!

In one extreme or the other BOTH cause many to be in error, fall away, and compromise in one way or the other. One extreme is over cautions about ANY TYPE of spiritual experience that is at all supernatural, spiritual, powerful, or miraculous. They run away from visions, dreams, any visitations from angels or Jesus, any demonic deliverance, healings, or the Baptism in the Spirit. Not to mention speaking in tongues! These people relegate everything to the Christian life to being sinful people being "tamed" to keep up a moral life and doing what's right and integral. But run away from anything that's out of your natural man's control!

Listen closely. That's an extreme that's going to send multitudes to Hell! It is selfish, natural, prideful, and it's a form of religion that's absolutely denying the power of the Gospel to free them. It's sad to me. These folks are not even born again! Born again comes from a person being "drawn by the Spirit" to the Lord. That Spirit convicts you of being in sin. You repent, die to yourself, and declare that Jesus is Lord over every single part of your life! That means that you submit all of your natural life, your inner and your outer life, - all to an invisible God. That's when an invisible Spirit transforms your inner man! He does something supernatural and creates within you a new man! You get baptized in water and the Spirit continues to change your whole inner man! You declare that Jesus is your Lord to all the World! Jesus, the Father, and the angels celebrate you!

Heaven Awaits Your Expression

You, a sinner that repents, are celebrated by the Heavens! Then you are new! Old things are passed away and behold all things are new and of God. You seek God and He fills you with His Holy Spirit!

You are like a brand-new baby that comes out of the womb and you babble and cry! You speak a new language! The language from Heaven! You are now sealed and stamped with a new citizenship! The Heavenly Jerusalem is your home city! You are of the Family of God Jehovah! You are a younger brother or sister to the Lord Jesus Christ! You now have His Spirit, His name, His Word, His Mission, His Mind, Your His body, you have His Father, and His inheritance! All of Heaven is Your Inheritance and so is the Earth! You are joint heirs with Jesus Christ!

You are now positioned as a son of God, and anointed into that position, and you now have a purpose! You are destined to be conformed into the image of Jesus! You have His purpose to fulfill all righteousness on the Earth and do what pleases your Heavenly Father!

That's the truth of the matter. That's very spiritual, very supernatural, and very powerful! That's the truth of the Word of God. That's the straight and the narrow. Jesus showed us how to live this life as a son. Jesus and His disciples are our example.

Jesus had angels appear to him.

Peter and all the disciples had angelic visitations.

Paul had angelic visitations.

John did as well. He gave us the Book of Revelation.

Every one of those healed the sick, cast out demons, raised the dead, had visions, had dreams, and experienced the presence of God Almighty.

This is what we see in the Word of God. We see even more supernatural things in the Book of Acts. Philip was translated from one city to another (Acts 8:39)! Ananias & Saphira dropped dead for lying to the Lord (Acts 5)! Paul was bitten by a snake and he didn't die (Acts 28)! Guys, if you read your Bible you will see the straight and narrow truth of what a believer's/disciple's life should look like.

Heaven Awaits Your Expression

Remember, we must interpret our experiences **by the word of God** and not interpret the word of God **by our experiences**. Just because you are still in sin doesn't mean the Word of God doesn't mean what it means. It says you are free from sin. Just because you can point to evidence of sin around you doesn't mean the Word isn't true!

You've never seen anyone healed? Does that mean the Word of God doesn't mean what it means about healing? Did Jesus, who is the express image of the nature of God, only heal people metaphorically? No, that's absurd. Salvation is real. The New Man is real. Heaven is Real. Hell is real. Satan and demons are real. Healing is real. Sin is real.

It is time to wake up. Seriously, open your eyes and see the world around you and the world that you can't see. It's time to acknowledge that God is the Creator of everything you see. He has catalogued a lot of His acts within the Bible for you to discover Him all you want!

I would say that's our final authority- **the Word of God**. For sons of God, that's how we discover what to believe and what not to believe. You can find understanding by knowing the Lord and letting Him teach you.

Back to the extremes within the Body of Christ about miracles and the supernatural.

The other extreme is just as dangerous. They build whole ministries, whole movements, and whole cultures based upon nothing but the supernatural experiences. This extreme is currently very popular around the world. These stress hours and hours of worship and esteem the feelings of the Presence of God experiences. They idolize miracles, visions, dreams, worship leaders, and much more. You will see far too many examples of exalting leaders to the forefront based solely upon the "anointing, the miracles, the talent, the visions, the angels, the glory, the power, etc." and then neglect the weightier matters of our calling like repentance from sin, godly character, integrity, modesty, purity, honesty, the fruit of the Spirit in all things, accountability to leaders, and obedience to the Lord in living right all the way til the day we die! Far too often, you will hear Grace as the reason they can still live like the World and do miracles in the name of Jesus on Sunday.

These same leaders tend to join to quickly to celebrities who decide to "add Jesus" to their line of products and fame.

Take Kanye West as an example and Justin Bieber. A lot of these leaders were shouting on the rooftops how the Body of Christ should receive these too into the fold. That of course has its proper place. Right. Anyone who repents and makes Jesus Lord has their place within the Body of Christ.

But they go as far as to stand and endorse these celebrities to preach, pastor, and lead in this "revival" they call it. Forget what Jesus said about iniquity. Jesus said we know people by their fruit. When you see the fruit of these celebrities you see them touting as the next leaders in the last great reformation- you will vomit.

This is an extreme. You don't get approval from God just by operating in the Spirit and doing miracles in the name of Jesus. You GET to do that. But if you want to enter into Heaven, you must be living right. You must depart from iniquity and still be loving others and doing things for Him. You must be doing both. That's the middle of the road. That's solid doctrine. That's the Bride Jesus is coming back for.

All of the supernatural things are clearly in scripture, are they not? Of course, they are, but you can't neglect one side and run to the other.

This scripture says it all:

Matt 7:21-23
>**21 Not every one that saith unto me, Lord, Lord, shall enter into the kingdom of Heaven; but <u>he that doeth the will of my Father</u> which is in Heaven.**
>
>**22 <u>Many will say</u> to me in that day, Lord, Lord, have we not prophesied in thy name? and in thy name have cast out devils? and in thy name done many wonderful works?**
>
>**23 And then will I profess unto them, <u>I never knew you: depart from me, ye that work iniquity</u>.**

Jesus said clearly that not everyone that says to Him "Lord, Lord" will enter into His Kingdom! Many will say to Him on that dreadful day, "Didn't we prophesy?

Didn't we do miracles, preach, sing, and experience Your presence? Didn't we do many great things in Your Name?"

Jesus said He would look at them and command them to depart from Him because they were still workers of iniquity!!! He said they would not make it into the Kingdom of Heaven on the Day of Judgment if they only stayed on one side of the spectrum and not do both. He wants us to live right and depart from iniquity AND to do the supernatural wondrous things in His name! We must do BOTH! That's the middle of the line, the straight and the narrow, or like I say, "**the Biblically Whole Approach**" to this matter.

You can't say to me, "Brock, see, it says not to do miracles there in that scripture! It says to just depart from iniquity." That's not what He was saying! He clearly wants us to do the same works He did. He commanded His disciples to do the same works He did. In Acts, we see that they obeyed Him and did the same as Jesus did! We must depart from iniquity AND still love and serve those around us!

Let's take this time and read what is expected of you before you stand before Jesus on that great and dreadful day:

Matthew 25: 31-46

31 When the Son of man shall come in his glory, and all the holy angels with him, then shall he sit upon the throne of his glory:

32 And before him shall be gathered all nations: and he shall separate them one from another, as a shepherd divideth his sheep from the goats:

33 And he shall set the sheep on his right hand, but the goats on the left.

34 Then shall the King say unto them on his right hand, Come, ye blessed of my Father, <u>inherit the kingdom prepared for you</u> from the foundation of the world:

35 For I was an hungred, and ye gave me meat: I was thirsty, and ye gave me drink: I was a stranger, and ye took me in:

36 Naked, and ye clothed me: I was sick, and ye visited me: I was in prison, and ye came unto me.

37 Then shall the righteous answer him, saying, Lord, when saw we thee an hungred, and fed thee? or thirsty, and gave thee drink?

38 When saw we thee a stranger, and took thee in? or naked, and clothed thee?

39 Or when saw we thee sick, or in prison, and came unto thee?

40 And the King shall answer and say unto them, Verily I say unto you, <u>Inasmuch as ye have done it unto one of the least of these my brethren, ye have done it unto me</u>.

41 Then shall he say also unto them on the left hand, Depart from me, ye cursed, into everlasting fire, prepared for the devil and his angels:

42 For I was an hungred, and ye gave me no meat: I was thirsty, and ye gave me no drink:

43 I was a stranger, and ye took me not in: naked, and ye clothed me not: sick, and in prison, and ye visited me not.

44 Then shall they also answer him, saying, Lord, when saw we thee an hungred, or athirst, or a stranger, or naked, or sick, or in prison, and did not minister unto thee?

45 Then shall he answer them, saying, Verily I say unto you, Inasmuch as ye did it not to one of the least of these, ye did it not to me.

46 And these shall go away into everlasting punishment: but the righteous into life eternal.

Heaven Awaits Your Expression

You see, it's believing His words and obeying Him. We are to Love Him with all our heart, mind, soul, & strength by loving Him through all the others we love and serve.

As He has loved us, we are to love others with the same love He has given to us. When you love and serve others as a son of God, you will grow in your abilities to meet more and more needs. If you look at the fullest example of a son of God, then you will see Jesus Christ Himself. He is our example of a son walking in the fullness of the Spirit on the Earth. He demonstrated a life of one who could meet any need that came before Him. He loved the sinners, forgave them, he healed the sick, cast out demons, cleansed the lepers, raised the dead, calmed storms, walked on water, changed water to wine, fed the hungry, taught of Heaven, and even loved all the children. Jesus had godly character, was honest in all He did, lived in perfect wisdom, was pure, holy, sanctified, consecrated, knew proper doctrine, and was a Spirit filled leader. Jesus properly lived both sides properly for us to see! Jesus showed us the example! He lived free from sin and served others! That's what we are to do. Depart from iniquity and serve others. You can't have one without the other. That's it. Love God by living clean and by serving others in love.

This is a life and death matter. Hell, or Heaven, is the result of your decisions today. Not to mention those who watch you and learn from your example.

Heaven Awaits Your Expression

CHAPTER 12

THE LIBRARY OF WISDOM

"I looked up where the roof should be and there were all the angels standing in attention in the sky around Jesus and myself."

Once I recovered from the Glory of Jesus, I looked toward Him again, only to see his feet. Yes, His feet! He was barefoot and walking on the perfectly green grass. The grass seemed to bow down before His feet in the exact place where His feet would step. It was such a powerful display of how EVEN THE GRASS obeys and has its place here in Heaven!

I literally had a whole new moment with the Lord just staring at His feet walking through the grass. I had another time altering, soul renewing, and revelatory transformation. Yes. Just by looking at His feet. He spoke so much scripture to me inwardly in that moment. I want to spare you all the time-consuming details of that moment. He taught me more in a few seconds considering His feet than I've learned from reading whole books on the Earth.

In summary, He taught me about the feet of those who carry glad tidings. He quoted to me the portion where Moses was told to take his shoe off.

Then Joshua was told to honor the ground and be bare foot as well. He called this Holy Ground. He quoted Psalms 37 and said that the steps of a good man are "ordered by the Lord."

Heaven Awaits Your Expression

He taught me to interpret that differently now that I'm a son of God. It's not just that our steps are ordered, as in being directed and told where to Step. I was originally seeing that scripture as meaning, "Everywhere I go and everything I do was predetermined and destined by God. God decides where I go, what I do, and to where I step. He leads and guides the steps of a good man." I think that's the consensus of every preacher I've ever heard preaching with that scripture. But I obviously didn't have the full Heavenly picture!

Jesus broke it down. I was like the men who walked by Jesus on the road and their hearts BURNED within them. Just hearing Jesus break down a scripture to you was making my insides burst in every direction! It was thrilling!

Jesus explained to me that Him and I are one. His authority is inside of me. He has given me the keys to the kingdom of Heaven. What I bind on Earth is bound in Heaven. He was telling me that the Kingdom of God is within me. He quoted that where the souls of my feet tread, that has been given to Me as a joint heir of the Lord. The Earth is the Lords and the fullness thereof. He went on to say that because I'm a son, that's my place in the order of things. The world has been ordered by the Lord.

It was becoming clear now. I was in my place within the order of the world. God the Father, His firstborn Son Jesus Christ, and then all those sons who are one with Jesus. These all were positioned in the order far above all principality and power and dominion and every name that is named in this world and the one to come. The Father has placed all things under His feet, and we are His body- one with Him. We are in the authoritative order of all things. We were (past tense) raised with Him and seated with Him in Heavenly places. (Ephesians 1 & 2)

He was quoting Matthew 28 where Jesus declared that "all power in Heaven and in Earth was given to Him" and then He said to me, "Brock, everywhere you go it declares the order of God.

It has been ordered by the Lord that you are representing Him in that very spot you walk.

You are ordered with that position in the order of things and therefore have that responsibility to step accordingly. Notice that it did not say, "the steps of all men are ordered by the Lord."

He paused, and reiterated, "It doesn't say the steps of a bad man are ordered by the Lord either."

He then drove it in, "It is because the good man was stepping and doing good. That is why it says it was ordered of the Lord. He was doing good and doing what was ordered by the Lord. The Lord orders His sons to do good. His sons are within the order of the world to DO GOOD wherever they go. When a son is doing good everywhere, they are doing what is ORDERED. Sons of God will be conformed into the Image of Jesus and do what Jesus does and what Jesus orders. That's the order of my Kingdom and that's WHAT I've ordered. Sons of God who are good men doing good things are ordered by the Lord to do that. That is what the feet of my sons do. They step and do as is ordered within their order- to do good as a man. He quoted the scripture as it is recorded:

Psalms 37:23

23 The steps of a good man are <u>ordered</u> by the Lord: and he delighteth in his way."

He smiled and said, "You can read this both ways."

He quotes it backwards, saying, "The Lord, by Him, comes order and orders, to all that are men, to be good and do good with all their steps. When you do this, I delight in your ways. Or you can read it just as it is and read, "The steps of a good man are ordered by the Lord: and he delighteth in his way." If you see this the way I say it, then you will, know who you are in Me in the order of all things, what your orders are, and then obey them every step."

WOW. WOW. WOW.

That's when I lost it again.

I was never going to read the Bible the same again.

Heaven Awaits Your Expression

I was going to forever depend on the Author Himself to guide me into all truth and teach me how to live!!!

Oh, I was full to overflowing with fire from the altar!

I was having a master bible training with Jesus Himself. I was thinking of Jesus sitting in the temple with the teachers, scribes, & rabbis when He was only 12 years old and confounding the wisest in the land.

I was confounded and knew I would never be the same.

~

I was made to look up. I looked and took in the details of this huge library before me. The pillars were made of a golden ivory with tints and shades of gold I can't describe. It was the most beautiful ivory gold marble stone you can imagine. It stood for what had to me many thousands of feet tall. I can't even describe the dimensions anymore. I seem to have lost translation on some details of exact dimensions I knew to be fact there. I knew dimensions of everything I saw there. But here, I can't tell if it was 10,000 feet or two miles. I just know they were HUGE. These pillars stood out to me again because there were no pieces of rock, no marks of hammer chiseling, it was one perfectly designed slab of stone. The whole library seemed to be one stone. Amazing. The library went for at least 80 miles (I think I remembered that much).

~

Disclaimer: Most of my experience in Heaven was written down in the moment. This experience at the Library was the one case where I tried to go back afterwards and type my memories. It got difficult to write after the experience with the Glory of Jesus! I lost track of keeping up with my writing.

~

So, back to the library.

There was no roof to this library. There were no walls. Just pillars and pillars and pillars.

Heaven Awaits Your Expression

I guess there's no rust, not moth, no deteriorating of books over time in Heaven. Only on Earth does material fade away, rush, mold, and fade. Here, everything stays in its perfect state for eternity.

There were shelves of books near the center of the library. The library was probably a few football fields wide. Inside, near the middle of the library were golden shelves and diamond shelves. I can't even tell you if it really was shelves there. It seemed as such. The only detail I remember was seeing old books of different sizes. Some were larger than me, and others were small as in a foot tall. Some were probably 10 ft tall or more. I just know that there were books and books as far as you can see. I saw the book ends only. So, were they all books? Were some scrolls? Not entirely sure.

I looked up where the roof should be and there were all the angels standing in attention in the sky around Jesus and myself. My guardian angel was to my back left and the scribe angel to my back right. Angels were everywhere. It was seeming kind of a formal presentation to Jesus.

I wondered at how many angels there could be standing at attention. I could see angels standing at attention above the library as far as I could see. I only looked quickly in both directions of the library.

I calculated where we were in the City of Heaven. We seemed to be near the far-right side of the library. What I mean is, the Father's throne and Person was near my back left. The part of the library that was furthest from The Father. That's what I mean. We were standing between the Father's light and the library. The Father seemed to be much closer here than where I started this journey off by the water at the veil of Heaven. I was in an area of angelic work. This area reminded me of being in DC where everything is federal buildings. This was an area of Kingdom work.

I kept looking up at these angels. I was in awe of how they could stand so still in the sky. I mean, wouldn't they drift a bit? They would not even move a muscle. I was thinking of movies and people flying on jet packs. They couldn't stay that still. These angels seemed to stand on something invisible.

But what do I know! They were standing there in attention like ancient statues. Works of art. Employees honoring their boss. Soldiers at attention before their Commander in Chief. They were doing exactly that!

That's it!

They were the workers who had a job to do. They were in the army of the Hosts of Heaven. These were not looking like the warrior guardian angel I had standing to my left though. These angels were not as warrior like, but warriors none the less.

Then Jesus began to clarify, "Brock, these are the angels that bring wisdom to My people. When they need an answer, wisdom, or knowledge about anything they can't acquire within their reach- these are the angels who deliver the messages. These angels are not the guardians that you just thought of. These only leave on assignment. They are not assigned to just one person. Just assigned. Remember, what I've said about my angels:

Hebrews 1:14

14 Are they not all ministering spirits, sent forth to <u>minister for them who shall be heirs of salvation</u>?

Job 1:10

10 Hast not thou <u>made an hedge about him</u> (angels surrounding Job's property), and about his house, and about all that he hath <u>on every side</u>? (Angels around everything Job owned) Thou hast blessed the work of his hands, and his substance is increased in the land.

Psalm 91:11-12

11 For he shall give his angels charge over thee, <u>to keep thee in all thy ways</u>.

12 They shall <u>bear thee up in their hands</u>, lest thou dash thy foot against a stone.

Heaven Awaits Your Expression

Jesus said,

> *"All of the angels you see in Heaven are sent on assignments to serve those who are heirs of my kingdom. They protect, they fight, they bring anything I need done to my People."*

Jesus continued, "These angels you see before you are the angels that work with Gabriel. Gabriel is My archangel over these who carry wisdom and messages to My people. They take what is here and deliver it to you when you ask. Remember Daniel? Mary? Zachariah?"

Then, of course, I remembered all the scripture references immediately:

Daniel 9: 21-23 to (the prophet Daniel)

21 Yea, whiles I was speaking in prayer, even the man <u>Gabriel</u>, whom I had seen in the vision at the beginning, being <u>caused to fly swiftly</u>, touched me about the time of the evening oblation.

22 And he informed me, and talked with me, and said, O Daniel, I am now come forth to give thee skill and understanding.

23 <u>At the beginning of thy supplications</u> the commandment came forth *(Jesus ordered the angel Gabriel on assignment)*, and I am come to shew thee; for thou art greatly beloved: therefore understand the matter, and consider the vision.

Daniel 8: 15-16 to (the prophet Daniel)

15 And it came to pass, when I, even I Daniel, had seen the vision, and sought for the meaning, then, behold, there stood before me as the appearance of a man.

> **16 And I heard a man's voice between the banks of Ulai, which called, and said, <u>Gabriel, make this man to understand the vision</u>.** *(Perhaps that was Jesus again?)*

> **Luke 1:18 to (Zacharias the father of John the Baptist)**
> **18 And Zacharias said unto the angel, Whereby shall I know this? for I am an old man, and my wife well stricken in years.**
> **19 And the angel answering said unto him, <u>I am Gabriel</u>, that stand in the presence of God; and am sent to speak unto thee, and to shew thee these glad tidings.**

> **Luke 1: 26-28 to (Mary the mother of Jesus)**
> **26 And in the sixth month the <u>angel Gabriel was sent from God</u> unto a city of Galilee, named Nazareth,**
> **27 To a virgin espoused to a man whose name was Joseph, of the house of David; and the virgin's name was Mary.**
> **28 And the angel came in unto her, and said, Hail, thou that art highly favoured, the Lord is with thee: blessed art thou among women.**

Jesus continued, "Brock, you can see that Gabriel brings the wisdom, messages, & understanding to those to my people as needed. These angels all work with him. He has sent many angels to my people to guide them day by day."

Then, like always, scripture is always flowing through me as Jesus would speak. I was seeing every reference to angels I've read in the Bible before my mind. I saw all of the following scriptures in such quick succession:

> **Acts 27: 21-25 (the apostle Paul on a ship in a bad storm)**
> **21 But after long abstinence Paul stood forth in the midst of them, and said, Sirs, ye should have hearkened unto me, and not have loosed from Crete, and to have gained this harm and loss.**

22 And now I exhort you to be of good cheer: for there shall be no loss of any man's life among you, but of the ship.

23 For there <u>stood by me this night the angel of God, whose I am, and whom I serve,</u>

24 Saying, Fear not, Paul; thou must be brought before Caesar: and, lo, God hath given thee all them that sail with thee.

25 Wherefore, sirs, be of good cheer: for I believe God, that it shall be even as it was told me.

Matthew 1:20 (angel appears to Joseph in a dream)

20 But while he thought on these things, behold, the angel of the Lord appeared unto him in a dream, saying, Joseph, thou son of David, fear not to take unto thee Mary thy wife: for that which is conceived in her is of the Holy Ghost.

Matthew 28: 1-7 (angel rolled back the stone)

1 In the end of the sabbath, as it began to dawn toward the first day of the week, came Mary Magdalene and the other Mary to see the sepulchre.

2 And, behold, there was a great Earthquake: <u>for the angel of the Lord descended from Heaven, and came and rolled back the stone from the door, and sat upon it.</u>

3 His countenance <u>was like lightning, and his raiment white as snow</u>:

4 And for fear of him the keepers did shake, and <u>became as dead men</u>.

5 And the angel answered and said unto the women, Fear not ye: for I know that ye seek Jesus, which was crucified.

6 He is not here: for he is risen, as he said. Come, see the place where the Lord lay.

7 And go quickly, and tell his disciples that he is risen from the dead; and, behold, he goeth before you into Galilee; there shall ye see him: lo, I have told you.

Acts 5: 18-20 (The apostles)
18 And laid their hands on the apostles, and put them in the common prison.
19 But <u>the angel of the Lord by night opened the prison doors,</u> and brought them forth, and said,
20 Go, stand and speak in the temple to the people all the words of this life.

Acts 8: 26 (Phillip)
26 And <u>the angel of the Lord spake unto Philip</u>, saying, Arise, and go toward the south unto the way that goeth down from Jerusalem unto Gaza, which is desert.

Acts 10: 3 (Cornelius)
3 He saw in a vision evidently about the ninth hour of the day an angel of God coming in to him, and saying unto him, Cornelius.

Acts 12:7-8 (Peter released from prison)
7 And, behold, the angel of the Lord came upon him, and a light shined in the prison: and he smote Peter on the side, and raised him up, saying, Arise up quickly. And his chains fell off from his hands.
8 And the angel said unto him, Gird thyself, and bind on thy sandals. And so he did. And he saith unto him, Cast thy garment about thee, and follow me.

Heaven Awaits Your Expression

Jesus continued, "Brock, anything you need is here. I own it all. Everything you see on Earth or in Heaven is mine.

You should never doubt my ability to accomplish my will through you. My Spirit is in you as well as these angels. Whatever you need, you have access through My Spirit. Now, come inside and sit at that table."

I was up and walking in an instant. I saw this massive solid golden ivory granite table with the same stone as a bench to sit upon. I was still moving toward the table and stepped over the stone to sit down and my only thought was, "Oh my that's going to be uncomfortable."

You see, on Earth, I can't stand to sit on rock hard objects! I get very uncomfortable and end up standing instead. Well, that was the thought I had.

But when I began to sit on the stone bench, it actually caressed my buttocks and was quite pleasant! It was very comfortable. I wasn't thinking much on this once after I sat down because I was noticing all the books ahead of me. On the sides of the books were written symbols of what I knew to be the language of God. I knew it was.

Standing to the far left in attention was the brightest angel I've ever seen. He still radiated a light like that of the time when we all were caught up in the euphoria of Jesus glorifying Himself with blinding light. This angel seemed to still be lightning white, His skin look like shiny instrumental brass under a spotlight. Picture a man playing a saxophone and his instrument is polished and shining so bright and radiating with the spotlight on it. It was brass on fire! Imagine brass that's shining but had a star underneath and the light was shining out of the brass from within. It was the skin of the angel Gabriel!

He was standing tall and was like no other angle I've seen yet. He was shining in a glory a lot like that of Jesus but obviously not like His entirely. I wondered at His golden bright hair, his hot molten golden or brass skin (you couldn't tell what color his skin was with all the light!), his pure lightning white robe, and the most amazing golden sash around his waist. He had something around his neck and chest that radiated in a colorful vesture of all colors reflected in Heaven.

Heaven Awaits Your Expression

I think that chest plate was giving off all the colors represented in Heaven. It was something like the ephod you read about in the Bible that the priests wore to commune with God.

This Gabriel started to loosen up the starlight show and began to look at me and become bearable to look at.

Jesus began to speak within me asserting, "Brock, Gabriel is shining and radiating the expression I created him to give for no other reason than Me standing here and talking about him to you. I was giving Him honor. Anytime I mention the work of Gabriel on the Earth, He turns glorious to behold. When we appeared here at the Library of Wisdom, I honored them by radiating my Presence to them. That's why they all shined brighter than the sky as we approached. Now Gabriel and his crew have an assignment. They must bring you the book you choose. Now choose any book you wish."

I was like, "Oh ok, let's choose that one!" I did all of this instinctively and definitely a bit like the new kid on the block standing in front of the biggest kids on the school yard I've ever seen. I was not hiding my trembling being. I was in a sheer, out of my comfort zone, nervous bit before all of these beings. I pointed at the one that came to mind.

An angel came down from standing on thin air, landed by the book, had the book instantly within its arms, and appeared before me. He opened his arms and held out the book for me to read the front cover. It was about 2 feet tall and wide. It was as thick as my whole hand and had a rustic eternal look to it. It didn't look old; it just looks like it was created before time and had no Earthly letter or symbol on it. It wasn't made of leather. It seemed to be made of some kind of stone like wooden material. Was the book cover made of stone or wood? I have no clue. It didn't make a difference to me because I remembered seeing trees that looked like stone in the city! So, I didn't think too much on that.

It had huge ancient letters/symbols on it. My only thought was an ancient Hebrew. But I never finished my thoughts.

Heaven Awaits Your Expression

Jesus commanded the angel to bring the book. He did. He grabbed the book on both sides and laid it down before me. It laid there on the huge table in front of me unopened.

I asked the Lord, "What do these symbols mean?"

He said, "That's the language of God. You will be able to read that when you come here for eternity. It says, "Frequency Infused Water.""

I looked at the book and repeated slowly, "Frequency Infused Water?"

He nodded and said, "Read."

I immediately opened it up and the first page had sentences like thoughts of my own. It was me discovering about how to infuse water with frequencies in order to keep the water clean. I read on.

It said, "By taking a thin line and running it through the water on your farm, you can emit a radio frequency and energize the water a lot like it is here in Heaven. You will notice that the plant life will respond much better to the water that's alive with the infused water. The cows, chickens, sheep, & other livestock will thrive on the water. You will discover that they will drink less water than they have drank historically."

I looked at the illustrations on the book became video before my eyes. I was envisioning all of this like it was my idea. I was seeing news articles and documentaries proclaiming that the large meat industry was using up too much of the world's water supply in much of the world. The solution came to me in the vision. We could infuse the water and the cattle would drink less."

Then I turned the page. The next page brought up scriptures in the Book of Revelation where it said 1/3 of the world would die due to bitter water. I read that Satan has plans to use evil people to poison the underground aquifers below major cities, suburbs, and small country cities. The city water supplies would be poisoned and so would the country folk's water underground. The country folk depended on their well water, spring water, etc. I saw the water being poisoned through long pipes going into the Earth and gases, chemicals, etc. being released into the Earth under the guise of a good cause.

(Not sure if that's what we call "fracking" or not- but it sure sounds a lot like the fracking process I've researched. Google Flint Michigan water and Flint Michigan Fracking).

I saw further through the next illustration/video that we could pipe down the same conduit line down into the aquifers from where the well water is pulled from and infuse it with a frequency that would kill the harmful bacteria and poison.

I saw how farmers could implement the same concept into the irrigation system for orchards, gardens, and landscaping. I saw the same radio frequency being able to affect the plants within a garden by playing out loud within certain types of music. I was seeing a garden of mine in the future where I would have the outdoor rock speakers playing out within my gardens. It would be playing a beautiful serenading worship music out within the plants. The plants would be watered with the infused water, hearing the worship music, and attracting the right insects and microbes to the farm.

I started to read on, but it seemed too exciting to not stop and ask Jesus permission. I asked Him, "Lord, should I continue reading?"

He actually told me to wait! He told me I would receive the rest when I needed it. I just figured He wanted me to read this little bit in order for me to share it with the world within this book.

~

It's been months after I had the visions in Heaven with the Lord. I've researched and looked up the infused water and found some amazing discoveries. I've yet to play the music out within our gardens. My family and I moved out into the mountains of Tennessee and are preparing new gardens. We fully plan to implement this into our next growing season! We trust that it's all for an appointed time. If you are an engineer, scientist, or a physicist and want to point me in the right direction on how to infuse water with radio frequencies, then by all means contact me and lets talk.

~

Heaven Awaits Your Expression

I was turning back to look at Jesus and there was no need. I appeared instantly to another portion of the library. I was on the far-left side that was closer to the Father's light.

Jesus began to tell me more about angels. He explained to me that I have two angels always with me. The guardian angel and the scribe angel. Everything I do is tracked, documented, and scribed within books. He said for me to know that every time I pray, I give my guardian angel work to do. He assured me that a guardian angel of his caliber deserves to be kept busy at all times. He sternly told me to never get stagnant, complacent, and lazy. I should always be watchful and be diligent to be about Our Father's Business.

I discovered that my mom has three angels with her mostly. She was blessed to be doing the works of a biblical widow detailed in 2 Timothy 5. There was an angel assigned to her at times to keep her from feeling lonely and to assist her in work. Since she was working for the kingdom, she was kept fully accompanied to stay the course. The Lord explained how that Him doing that was key to have me ready to begin my assignment. As Mary kicked Jesus out of the nest at the wedding in Cana, so too, my mom would see me catch fire.

My wife Laura has two angels watching her. I saw my son having two angels as well. I saw how my kids would each carry the assignment on the family as well. These angels were simply spirits sent to serve the people of God. They too were filled with the Spirit of God and were essentially all different moving parts within the army of God.

Jesus explained it to me like a typical Army in Heaven. There were soldiers on the grounds that were the actual shooters kicking down doors and rescuing hostages or POWs. There were those supporting them by driving the vehicles, flying the helicopters, flying the drones, flying the surveillance planes, flying the air support bombing jets, those working the communications and logistics in a command location, many sailors on a ship providing support, many sailors in submarines providing intelligence, satellites in space, many offices in a few countries working different angles, and many different civilian manufacturers who make the weapons, clothes, and equipment.

The list could go on and on to about how much support goes on just for the foot soldier to do his job. I was getting His point.

Jesus made it very clear. Roger that. 10-4. He had many moving parts within His kingdom to ensure that me and other believers can do the mission effectively. The one thing he lacked - LABORERS. He told me that soldiers need to enlist. Soldiers need to do a job. Soldiers need to be busy. His people need to do the Great Commission and Love God with all their heart, mind, soul, & strength.

As if Jesus was perfectly on cue, out came a sonic boom from the sky across the way. About a half mile or so, was a fireball bursting into my sight. It was an impressive fireball. A ball of light. It was what looked like what I've seen time and time again as a cylinder round light- looking like what people have called UFO's. Yep. Picture a sonic boom a jet makes when it hits the sound barrier. It's a round ball of light. You should YouTube a jet going sonic boom. Actually, it was way too many light explosions, or sonic booms, for me to count- even with my Heavenly mind. Maybe I could if I tried. I was way too thrilled and startled to count. Hundreds of thousands of sonic booms just happened before me in the distance!

Well, that's what the huge angels just displayed as they came into my vision. I noticed that they did this on purpose. They slowed down to the speed of sound for me to see them. It seems the Lord had me see this.

These were the biggest angels I've seen yet! They had to be 20 feet tall! These were huge muscular terrifying angels! Jesus was implanting knowledge into me instantly. I knew the tall golden one at the top of the garrison of soldier angels was Michael himself. What a sight to see. I knew instantly that Michael and his angels were the warring soldier angels. No body messed with them. I could sense the angels around me paying their respects to Michael as he looked up at Jesus and myself.

Heaven Awaits Your Expression

"Whoa, Michael looked at me! What!" I said like a little schoolgirl at a concert. What was I saying? Oh, my word. I quickly got myself in line and payed my respects as the angels did around me.

I needed to learn the protocols here and learn them fast! I felt embarrassed to act out of line and not be in honor within the moment.

Jesus smiled inside. I could feel it. I was actually catching myself saying this as I watched Jesus hold His hand up and out towards Michael and his angels. They had huge spears. Wait, those were swords! Good Lord Almighty! I have never seen such huge swords. These swords lit up on fire. It had to be hundreds of thousands- maybe millions or more swords lit up instantly and an amazing Earthquake shook the ground! Light from the Throne of God brightened instantly! The sound from the shaking was cracking in my ears and a push from the air hit my chest! These angels all did an instant bow. They all landed on their knees at the exact same time and it shook all of the region of Heaven I was at! It was the most impressive display of power I've ever seen! I've seen videos of North Korea, China, and Russia have huge military parades with soldiers marching and making every single step in complete unison. This was not even close. This was not a parade. This was just the angels coming back from a mission and instantly bowing in honor of their Commander in Chief- their King!

I found myself on my knee as well! Heck, I was not about to stand when those giants were on their knees! Heck no! I was down and feeling the power emanating out of Jesus, from the Father, and pulsating outwardly with what I could interpret as a pleasing gesture from the Throne! These giants instantly caused another BOOM. They must've all stood up with one smooth practiced motion. I looked up and that's exactly what they did. They were standing tall and shining in golden glory. Oh, now I see why the soldiers fell like dead people when a huge soldier angel moved that big rock out of the way and sat on the rock! Whew! I would've passed out too!

Jesus looked out and began to teach me, "Brock, these angels deal with Satan and his fallen angels head on every day. Satan can do nothing against them. Satan has been completely stripped of his dominion.

Heaven Awaits Your Expression

He is only a defeated foe who does nothing but fight through deception. He's the toothless lion roaring loudly making people think he can tear them to shreds with the teeth he doesn't have anymore.

He's just leading an insurgence force who does nothing but try to disrupt my occupying army on the Earth.

My sons and daughters are occupying until I come and make all things new. My Father knows the time and has prepared all things here for my return. It is near and will occur so fast, that no one will have time to prepare once they hear that loud sound barrier crack open in the Eastern sky. Just as you just heard Michael slow down to the speed of sound and there was a loud crack through all the skies. All of the universes will see and hear my Return. The light will pierce human bodies and expose skeletons. Sound and light will compete for atmosphere. I will be a terrible sight for those who don't know Me. I will speak and bodies will be no more. I will execute the plans of My Father and all the Earth will see me sit upon My throne in Jerusalem.

I will separate all the humans who's ever been conceived on Earth and pronounce judgment on each soul. Each individual will be held accountable for the work they've done within my great Eden. My vineyard has either had good work or evil. People have done the work that I've ordered or they've not. They've either scattered or gathered. They're either for Me or against Me. They are either a new creation or they're not. My new race of sons of God will know My coming and will run to the side of light. Those who don't know me will hide from the light. There will be great horrors on that day as people will scream as they disappear from sight. They will scream so horribly that you will hear the screams from hell even on top of the surface. There will weeping and gnashing of teeth.

For those who have obeyed Me, known Me, and trusted Me they will be received into My Father's Kingdom prepared from before Time. The angels will have the hardest assignment I've had to give them. They will go and reap the human harvest and separate them as I've commanded. It will be tough for any being full of My Spirit to witness.

Everyone will have the knowledge the Spirit gives. Everyone will know who is Mine and who is not. They will be marked."

This had me in such a silent frozen look. I couldn't believe what I was hearing. I've read things in the Word about His second coming, but never ever did I dream of hearing Jesus talk about it.

To hear Him discuss the realness and the pain of that Day had me in fear and trembling.

"Lord, what can I do? What can I do to help? What must I do? Oh Lord, don't let me be the reason anyone is separated away from you by the angels! Oh please! Oh, please let me be found without pride and without selfishness! Oh, let me be obedient in every area of my life! Let me be Biblically Whole and not a hypocrite! Let me be like You! Let me be AN EXAMPLE!" I was sobbing. I was dreadfully wailing before Him.

I had a deep travail hit me that poured out of me like I had the responsibility of the whole world on my shoulders! I felt like I would not be able to look Jesus in the eyes if I was the cause of just ONE PERSON screaming and being dragged into an eternal Hell! Oh no! Oh, let me be one that runs to the light! Let me be one that rides on a white horse beside my King! Oh, let me be one of His warriors that fights alongside the GIANT WARRING ANGELS! Oh, I wanted to be on the same team as those huge gigantic scary angels over there! I did NOT WANT TO FACE THEM!!!

Oh, I just looked at Jesus and He had a Kingly look on Him that told me there was no favorites. No respecting different people. NO favors. Absolutely no secrets to Him. It was the look of one who will do what is JUST and THAT'S IT. There was no grey area. There were no loopholes in this law. This was it. You were either a newly created race, a son of God, one of the royal priestly kings within His kingdom or you were not. You were either one that was born again and living right, or you were not. You either knew Him or not. It was clear to me. I wanted to be one who was born again, a new creation, loving God by living right and serving others. I would do whatever Jesus told me to do for the rest of my days and not shrink back. I was going to be found faithful till the end.

Heaven Awaits Your Expression

I would not be those who would trade in my birthright for a meal, like Esau did. I was not going to trade my eternity for fornication, lying, cowardliness, greed, hypocritical living, no mark of the Beast, no drugs, no witchcraft, no slander, gossip, or anything that didn't look like Jesus!

Jesus was going to be LORD AND KING of every area of my life and I was going to do what he willed without question.

I was determining that I would be ALL IN and SOLD OUT and DEAD TO ME. I would be fully dead to myself and take up my cross. There was no looking back now that I have my hand on the plow! I was going to overcome until the very end. I was going to offer my neck onto the guillotines or my hands and feet to the cross. I was going to die daily!

Jesus requires nothing less.

If you think Jesus will accept anything less than a dead self-less obedient son of God, then you have something coming. He requires that He be Lord of your life, you in obedience, and you departed from sin.

That is simple to do when you decide to be born again. You must decide RIGHT NOW that Jesus will be the complete master, king, and Lord of everything in your life. That's every single detail of your life. Your money, your dreams, your family, your job, your car, and yeah- ABSOLUTELY EVERYTHING.

If you lay all that down before the cross and decide once and for all that you will follow Him and obey Him in everything you learn from Him. You are doing what Jesus calls - REPENTING. You are changing your mind about every single thing in your life. You are choosing to think the WAY HE THINKS about each area of your life. You turn away from doing it your way and you do it HIS WAY ONLY.

That's repentance.

You can call out to the Lord and ask Him in your own words to forgive you of your sins, to come and make you a SON OF GOD. Ask Him to come and make you into a NEW CREATION.

Heaven Awaits Your Expression

When you do that, you can declare that He is your Lord out loud and to witnesses.

You should find someone to baptize you immediately so that you can obey the Lord and confess Him as your Lord before witnesses. IF you confess Him before men openly, then He will confess you openly before His Father and the angels.

You must be baptized and start your new life as a disciple. This life is an apprenticeship. Jesus himself send His Spirit into your spirit to lead you, guide you into all truth, and teach you all things. He is called to train you, mentor you, and coach you through your transformation into being like the firstborn Son of God. You have a new job now. Your position in the Family Business is that of a son. You are to start your on the job training as soon as you are born again. You are to start your training on how to Love God and how to Love People. You must find people who know God to go with them as the "GO" out and love others. You should find someone who truly knows God. You should be able to learn how to hear God speak to you, how to understand and study the Bible correctly, how to pray, how to discern what sin is, and know what righteousness looks like. You should know what the word says about who you are now as a new creation and know thoroughly everything the Bible says about Jesus Christ.

You should learn immediately how to do what Jesus commanded his disciples to do. You should accompany believers as they heal the sick, cast out devils, feed the hungry, comfort the orphans, visit widows, help the poor, visit the prisons, visit the hospitals, and love on anyone you can with the Love of God.

You should always be growing in your abilities to meet needs around you just like Jesus did. You should be able to be effective in having prayers answered. You should be fruitful. You should have a life that those around you should see a pattern of good works. Those around you should be able to predict in advance how you will behave or respond to a need that presents itself to you.

Heaven Awaits Your Expression

When you walk by a sick person, or a hungry person, or a depressed person those who know you should be able to predict how you will "meet the need" you just discovered.

You should be such a giver! You should learn in detail what the fruit of the Spirit are in Galatians 5.

You should be giving out love, joy, peace, patience, kindness, gentleness, goodness, faithfulness, & self-control in each and every interaction with another person. That's what we give out as Christians who walk in the Spirit. That's what we are doing when we give out healing, or money, or our time, our service, our knowledge, our words to comfort/encourage others, etc.

You should know that you have a responsibility as a son of God. Your response to His ability to meet a need is your response-ability. Responsibility is the area you will grow in as you grow in your knowledge of God and your experiences with Him. The more you obey Him consistently, the more responsibilities you take on as a son. It's a family business. The higher the position in the business, the more responsibility. The more responsibility, the more accountability. The more you are responsible, the less you have rights to have opinions. You die the more you go up. You must humble yourself to to grow in responsibilities. Your position will always stay the same. You are a son. A believer. A disciple. You are a son who serves. A bondservant. A servant who willfully chooses to be in service to your Master.

Your position is always going to be a son, who is serving as a disciple within his Father's Family business. Your assignment will change, however. You will be growing in responsibility and therefore have new assignments as your life goes on. You will lead others in different capacities. You will be tried and tested. You will have assignments of larger responsibility more and more as you go. This is the life of a son.

This is your life.

To all those who choose to be in the trenches with me. May the Love, Grace, & Life of Our Glorified King become real in every area of your life!

With Love, Brock & Laura Knight

HEAVEN AWAITS THE EXPRESSION
YOU WERE CREATED TO GIVE

Have you ever wondered what it is like to see Heaven, Jesus, or the Throne of God? What about the smells? Have you imagined the colors or pictured in your mind what an angel looks like? What will you do when the sheer power, light, and love of Jesus welcomes you into the veil of Heaven?

Join the author on a journey through the memoirs of his time in Heaven with The Father, Jesus, and the angels. Steady yourself to experience how the trees, flowers, rocks, grass, water, and all of God's Creation join together in the worship in Heaven.

Today, the disciples of Jesus Christ are facing the greatest prophetic moments of the ages. A believer must "seek those things which are above, where Christ sits at the right hand of God" (Col. 3:1-4) and "be changed into the same image from glory to glory" (2 Cor 3:18).

Discover how you were masterfully designed by your Creator to give your heavenly expression for such a time as this!

Brock, Laura, Daniel, Catalina, & Rocky had 2 months like no other. It was the beginning of 2020 and Brock was led by the Lord in prayer to be with Him for hours at a time. This book is the chronicles of those experiences in Heaven. The Knight Family now resides in the mountains of Tennessee. Brock is known as a believer, husband, father, business owner, author, reporter, pastor, & teacher. Brock is currently a White House Correspondent for WATB.tv working alongside his mother Dr. June Knight. Brock's greatest passion is to teach those around him to become like Jesus in every area of their lives.
Learn more at www.BiblicallyWhole.com

TreeHouse Publishers

Made in the USA
Columbia, SC
23 December 2020